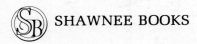 SHAWNEE BOOKS

Also in this series

THE MUSIC
CAME FIRST

The Memoirs of Theodore Paschedag

As Told to Thomas J. Hatton

SOUTHERN ILLINOIS UNIVERSITY PRESS
Carbondale and Edwardsville

Library of Congress Cataloging-in-Publication Data

Paschedag, Theodore, 1905–
    The music came first : the memoirs of Theodore Paschedag /
as told to Thomas J. Hatton.
        p.   cm.–(Shawnee books)
    1. Paschedag, Theodore, 1905–. 2. Conductors–United States–
Biography.   I. Hatton, Thomas J., 1935–.   II. Title.
ML422.P27A3 1988   87-28471
785'.092'4–dc19   CIP
[B]   MN
        ISBN 0-8093-1471-1. ISBN 0-8093-1472-X (pbk.)

Illustrations

P·R·E·F·A·C·E

I GOT TO KNOW Theodore Paschedag primarily through playing in the Southern Illinois Concert Band, which he directs. Before that time I had had brief encounters with him and had heard his name mentioned with respect in Southern Illinois music circles. I had shopped occasionally at the music store he owns in West Frankfort, and I had been present when the Herrin, Illinois, local of the American Federation of Musicians presented him with a plaque for outstanding service to music in the area.

When I began playing in the Concert Band, I quickly came to realize that Ted Paschedag is remarkable. Here was an energetic eighty-year-old who knew exactly what he wanted from the musicians before him and who was not going to settle for anything less. I was impressed with his dedication to the great band music of the past and the wit and humor that he used to teach those with no knowledge of it how it should be played. I saw that Ted is a man with a mission in life—nothing less than the revitalization of a musical tradition that many have given up for dead. Since I share his love for this tradition, I knew that I had found a kindred spirit.

I was also impressed with the respect and love that Ted inspired in his musicians. Several of these I found out had been his students thirty and even forty years ago. Others were the children and grandchildren of his former students. All of them were enthusiastic about once again playing under his baton. They took his criticism seriously and without rancor. They quite obviously considered being in his band a privilege. It must be a remarkable teacher, I thought, who can inspire such devotion after so many years.

Credit for the idea of this book must go to one of these former-student band members, Robert Treece. It was he who broached the subject to one of my colleagues in the English department of Southern Illinois University–Carbondale who contacted me. The basis for this memoir is a series of tape-recorded interviews Ted granted me throughout the summer and winter of 1983–84. They were almost all done in the kitchen of his home in West Frankfort, Illinois, as we sat across from each other at the little kitchen table. Now and then we would interrupt the tape to look at something from his extensive scrapbooks or listen to one of his many fine albums of band music. Occasionally, also, I would hit the "pause" button while we aired our similar ideas on musical and educational matters.

In writing this book I have made no attempt to reproduce any of these interviews verbatim, and I have edited and arranged material for logical and chronological consistency. I have, though, attempted to keep the flavor of Ted's narration as well as his point of view and his ideas. Not that a great deal of editing was necessary. Ted's memory is clear, and his mind is keen and logical. He tells his story well. In many, many instances I have used his own words with a minimum of editing.

Ted Paschedag's story is worth recording for a number of reasons. First, he is one of the last of a rapidly vanishing breed of musicians who played professionally before modern technology forever changed the nature of the music industry in the United States. The job of moving-picture theater musician ended almost overnight with the advent of talking pictures. Ted gives us a rare look at the world of the theater musician and the problems he faced when he was suddenly technologically unemployed. How he and his contemporaries dealt with their problems should certainly be of interest today when technological unemployment is ending hundreds of careers.

Secondly, Ted's memoirs give us an interesting insight into the early days of music education in the Midwest, and I suspect his experiences were not much different from those of pioneer music educators throughout the country. Ted Paschedag is living proof that Meredith Willson's *Music Man* is not pure fantasy. Here is a real-life music man who came to town to sell a children's band for a month and stayed on for over fifty years. His story is an important part of the history of music education in America, and the methods he used to achieve success are well worth looking at today.

Finally, Ted Paschedag is worth listening to because he is a wise man. I do not agree with all of the ideas he offers here on such subjects as music education, religion, culture, etc., although I find most of them pretty sensible. But here is a man who has been successful in several professions during one of the most stressful and constantly changing periods in the history of our country and is still bright and vigorous enough to make penetrating comments on what he experienced. The fact that he is also witty and entertaining with a sharp eye for the colorful anecdote and the incongurous irony makes hearing him a pleasure as well.

I would like to extend my gratitude to a number of people who have helped make this book possible. First, of course, I would like to thank Ted himself for those delightful sessions at his house and for his many other kindnesses to me. I would like to thank Bob Treece for initiating the project and for his help in reading the manuscript drafts. I would like to thank Bob, Bea Craig, La Verne Sanders, and Freda Pirtle for their comments on Ted's life. They gave me added insight into his character even though they were not ultimately included in this book. Finally, I must thank the Southern Illinois University Office of Research and Projects for the grant that helped to finance the writing of this work.

Thomas J. Hatton

THE MUSIC
CAME FIRST

O·N·E

I WAS BORN AUGUST 10, 1905, in St. Louis, Missouri. My father, William Paschedag, was an undertaker and also ran a livery stable. He was an amateur musician of sorts who played the bass drum. The Paschedag family is German, my grandfather having come from a small village near Hamburg. My mother, Lulu, was a Wilkinson, but her family was mostly French. I don't remember my father very well, because he died when I was only four years old. When this happened, my mother had to go to work at the Wagner Electric Company in St. Louis, and I went to live with my maternal grandmother, Amanda.

My grandmother was an excellent pianist and supported herself by giving lessons not only to beginners but also to many of the players who provided the background music for the silent movie theaters in St. Louis. Since these pianists were busy playing at the theaters during the afternoons and evenings, Grandmother usually started her lessons around midnight after the shows closed. Then she would continue into the small hours of the morning.

I'm sure it was because of my grandmother that I first acquired the love of music that has shaped my life. St. Louis was a center of musical activity in those years before World War I, and my grandmother's house on Kennerly Avenue was close to the heart of the city's show business district. It was the era of the concert band, and all the great bandleaders—Sousa, Pryor, Pat Conway, and the rest—brought their bands to town regularly. These organizations not only played what we would call concert music today but provided music for popular entertainment as well. I remember that one year when I was five or six the big popular hit was Sousa's "King Cotton" march. There were no stereos or even radios in those days, but almost every family had a player piano. That summer you could walk down the street on a warm evening and hear ten or fifteen player pianos going at once, all working away at different parts of "King Cotton."

We also lived not too far from the new Forest Park that had been made out of the St. Louis World's Fair grounds. What had been the Japanese pavilion at the fair had been turned into a bandstand, and it was there that the great bands gave evening and Sunday afternoon concerts. Almost as soon as I could walk my grandmother began taking me to these concerts.

"What kind of music is that?" she would ask me when the Pryor Band or the Sousa Band began a number.

"That's Chinese music, Grandma," I would answer, or "That's an Irish jig," or "That's a polka." I learned to identify these musical types long before I could spell their names.

Shortly after I came to live with her, Grandmother decided that it was time for me to learn to play the piano, so she started assigning me little lessons with scales and simple tunes. With her the music always came first. No matter what other activities I had before me, I first had to get my piano lesson practiced. Even after I started school and had homework, it was always first the piano, then the schoolwork. In the summer she would have me get up at four o'clock in the morning, practice a couple of hours, have breakfast, and then practice for another hour. Then I could go outside and play.

"The music comes first." I guess that's been the guiding principle in my life to this day. That was the tradition in the Old Country among the people from which I came. They believed that art—music especially—was the foundation for all learning. One first developed a knowledge and love for culture, and this would lead one to a desire for intellectual attain-

4

ment in general. Art was not just a frill; it was the basis for all true education.

You might think that with all the practicing I would have rebelled against the grind. The truth is, though, I loved it. On nights that I could stay up late Grandmother would often let me sit in on the piano lessons that she gave. I had a little rocking chair, and even though it was after midnight, I would take my chair and sit quietly listening as Grandmother worked with her pupils. I can still remember many of the pieces they played, for there were many nights when I nodded off to sleep with that piano singing in my ears.

Of course, not everything I did was related to music. I guess I did most of the things that small boys of that time liked to do. I especially loved baseball. In those days we played baseball in the streets. The police were our friends back then, and we could usually get one of them to umpire for us. They didn't care where we played as long as three or four of us had a dime or a nickle or two in our pockets. This was in case we broke a window, for then we would all chip in and have it replaced. It took only thirty-five or forty cents to fix a broken window in those days.

Another source of excitement in my young life was the fire station on the corner of our block. This was the time of the horse-drawn fire wagon. Every night at nine o'clock our fire station had a practice. All of us children would gather outside the firehouse to hear the gong clang and watch the harnesses drop down on the big horses, and the firemen come sliding down the pole from their sleeping quarters on the second floor. Then off they would all go with the dogs barking, the children yelling, and the bell clanging away. With such a frenzy it was hard to go back home and climb into bed when the practice was over.

Our neighborhood was predominantly Irish Catholic even though my family was German and Protestant. When it came time for me to go to school, my grandmother decided to send me to St. Matthew's Parish School. It was right across the alley from our house, while to get to the public school I would have had to cross three streetcar tracks, and this was considered dangerous for a little fellow in those days. I went to that school until I started the fourth grade. Then my mother remarried, and I went to live with her and her new husband on a farm just outside of Labaddie, Missouri. At that time Labaddie was an almost 100 percent German community in the foothills of the Ozarks about forty miles west of St. Louis. "Labaddie" was the old German spelling of the name. Today the town spells it "Labadie."

Labaddie has always been surrounded by excellent farmland, and of course, the major business there was and is still today farming. Farming was very different when I lived there, for there were no tractors or mechanized farm machinery. The German farmers used little mules to pull their plows and wagons. I especially remember the threshing days in late summer, mainly because there was always an abundance of good food.

I went to a little country school in Labaddie that had only fourteen children from the first to the eighth grade. Shortly after I started, the school acquired a piano, and my mother would come and play it and teach the children to sing. I also continued my piano lessons with a teacher in town. It was about three miles from our farm to Labaddie, and on bad days I was allowed to make the journey on mule back. We had no saddle, but my Stepfather Shultz would throw a couple of gunny sacks over my mule Molly's back, and off I would go. Except that as soon as I got out of sight of home, I would get off and walk anyway, because Molly had a very sharp razor back.

When I got to Labaddie, I would often have to wait for the train, since my piano teacher came on it from the nearby town of Gray Summit. The train was often an hour or so late, and I had nothing to do but wander around the town. One establishment particularly attracted me. This was the *Labaddie Herald*, the town's weekly newspaper. For some reason it fascinated me to go and watch the girls there set type. This was long before the Linotype or the Monotype, and all the typesetting was done by hand.

One day as I was watching the setting, one of the girls called to me and asked if I would like to try my hand at it. I was more than willing. This girl let me come into the setting room and boosted me up on one of the high stools before the rows of type. Then she gave me a printer's stick and showed me how to set my name in print. After that I always hoped the train would be late so I could go down to the *Herald* and practice typesetting, and usually it was. Thus not only did I learn how to play the piano, but I also acquired a skill in printing that has stayed with me to this day.

I spent four years on the farm near Labaddie until I graduated from the eighth grade. Then the family decided that I should go back to St. Louis to go to high school. I was going to stay with my grandmother again, but before the school year started her youngest son died, and she went to California to be with his family. Luckily, my Aunt Emma and her family had returned to St. Louis from Panama, so I went to stay with them.

I went to Yateman High School in north St. Louis. At that time it was a school of about five hundred located just a block off Grand Avenue near Natural Bridge Road. High school was very different in those days. The discipline was much stricter, and the atmosphere was more serious than in today's schools. This was partly because the student body was more selective. Of all the students in St. Louis who completed grade school—and many didn't even get that far—only 50 percent went on. Of that 50 percent, only half would stay in high school after the end of the first year. The others would drop out either because they couldn't handle the studying or because they had to go to work or because of some reason or another. Of the few who did stay in school only 50 percent again would go on to graduation.

Thus high school was a place where you came to learn, and generally we were treated as adults. It was always, "Mr. Paschedag," "Miss Jones," and "Mr. Smith." If a teacher did condescend to use my Christian name, it was always "Theodore," never "Ted." And even though it was a public school, all the boys wore coats and ties. I remember once I forgot to put my tie on, and the assistant principal made me walk home and get it, a round-trip distance of some thirty blocks.

The European tradition of the importance of the arts was still adhered to at Yateman. Vocal music was a compulsory subject there. Our teacher was a Mrs. Dussuchal, and she taught us not only to sing but to study and appreciate the great arias from the operas and other types of classical music as

7

well. She was an excellent pianist, and she would tell us in her broken English, "You work hard, and on Friday I play you concert. I play you popular music which you like." And we would all work, because it was a real treat to hear her play.

Not that we didn't educate the body as well as the mind. Our music classes two days a week alternated with gym classes. Our gym teacher was Hans Lehrman, another first-generation German, who taught us intricate exercises and routines. Music and gym seemed to go together, and when in the spring Mr. Lehrman put on his gymnastic exhibitions for the parents, the high school orchestra would play background music for them.

I joined that orchestra as a flute player my freshman year. When I returned to St. Louis, I had begun going to the many silent movie houses around the city. In those days all the movie theaters had orchestras to provide background music for the pictures, and I used to love to watch the musicians as they played. Sometimes I would go to the same picture three or four times as much to hear the music as to see the show. For some reason the flutists appealed to me the most. I began to think that it would be a very fine thing to play one of those long wooden sticks in a theater orchestra someday.

As luck would have it, soon after I started classes at Yateman the orchestra director put out word that he needed a flutist. I immediately volunteered. The director gave me a flute, but it wasn't very good, so he went down town and got me a better one. Then he sent me to a flutist who had graduated the year before to take lessons.

At first I didn't make very much progress. The boy who was teaching me wasn't all that good himself, and even though I had had my piano lessons and knew music pretty well, it was slow going. In the meantime I continued to go to the theaters, and I would always try to get a seat down front as close to the flute player in the orchestra as possible. My favorite theater was the West End Lyric, mainly because it had an exceptionally fine flutist. Finally, I decided that if I was ever going to learn to play myself, I would have to get a better teacher, so I went to a music store and asked them to recommend a teacher. They suggested a Mr. John Sauter, who they said was

8

the best flute player in St. Louis. And Mr. Sauter turned out to be the same fine flutist that I had admired at the Lyric Theater for so long.

Mr. Sauter agreed to give me lessons, and after that I made progress more rapidly. He was an excellent teacher but a very demanding one. He lived in a third-floor flat on Ninth Street. He also owned a little dog. Another boy named Don Hampton and I used to go for our lessons together, and we always knew what to expect from Mr. Sauter even before we got to his apartment, because Mr. Sauter's dog would always meet us on the stairs. If the dog showed his teeth and growled at us, we knew that Sauter was in a bad mood and we were in for a rough lesson. If the dog wagged his tail and licked our hands, we could relax because his master was in a good mood and the lesson was going to go well.

On the whole, though, Sauter was very strict with us. This was because he was a professional musician, and he wanted us to be professionals.

"You want to be like me?" he would ask us. "You want to play in the theater like me? You have to practice and learn to read music perfectly. In the theater you have one rehearsal in the morning. You make a mistake, and the leader looks at you, but that's all right. You make that mistake again, though, and next day somebody else has your job. You never get a chance to make it a third time."

And later when I did play in the theaters I found out that that was the way it was. The leaders didn't accept sloppy playing or excuses. There were always two or three other musicians waiting for your job, and if you couldn't do it right, you got your two weeks' notice. But thanks to Mr. Sauter, I never got such a notice in my career, which was very unusual in those days.

Mr. Sauter taught me something else that has stayed with me to this day and carried over into my own teaching. Even though he could give me terrible tongue lashings, he always knew when to give a compliment or show some understanding. I remember one time when I had an especially bad lesson, mainly because I hadn't practiced much. Sauter really gave me hell; the dog was growling that day for sure. I went down those three flights of stairs nearly in tears muttering to myself about how I wasn't ever going to take another lesson from that old meany in my life.

I had to walk three blocks to the streetcar stop, and I stomped along feeling angry and hurt and stood on the corner, shoulders hunched, nose sniffing, waiting for the car for what I had determined would be the last time. Then suddenly I felt a big arm thrown round me. It was Mr. Sauter.

"You wait," he said. "You be all right. I still make you a fine flute player. Someday you'll be playing in the theater just like me."

Even though I was wrapped up in music in high school, I never lost my interest in printing. I used to like to stop and watch the printers at work on my walks to catch the streetcar after school. One day when my aunt and I were shopping I saw an ad in a store window for little handpresses you could send away for. Ten dollars was a lot of money, but I knew right away that I just had to have one of those presses. Then over Christmas vacation on the farm at Labaddie I was lucky enough to shoot a big old possom with my stepdad, and he gave the hide to me. The money I got from that was just enough to pay for the press.

I used my new prize to print up little odd jobs around my neighborhood, but I soon felt the need for more money. My family was having rough going, and I needed to pay for my flute lessons from Mr. Sauter by myself. Fortunately, one day I noticed that a new little printing shop, the Rapid Printing Company, had opened up on my way to the streetcar stop. I began to hang around this place watching the two men who ran it set type. Finally, one of them asked me if I was interested in printing, and when he found out that I could set type, he offered me a job. From then on I financed my flute lessons by setting print after school. My boss' name was Milo Reister, and his partner was a Mr. Boudis. I don't remember his first name, but everyone called him "Duck," I guess because he had a funny way of walking when he was a child.

In addition to the flute lessons, I also continued to play piano while in high school and was part of a little orchestra that played for the high school dances. It consisted of a violin, a saxophone, a cornet, and drums, and I played piano and directed. Every Friday afternoon the school held a two-hour dance after classes, and we made extra money playing for these. In those days we played marches and waltzes and polkas and that sort of thing for dancing, but anything that hinted of jazz or ragtime was considered improper. That was the time when "I Wish I Could Shimmy Like My Sister Kate," was popular, and our principal warned us that if he ever caught us playing that awful song, he'd fire us on the spot. Naturally, we had to play it, so we'd wait until we were sure that Mr. Fuller was not in the room and then we'd tear into "Sister Kate." Of course, one afternoon he caught us, but he was decent about it and let us off with a talking to.

By the time I graduated from high school I was both a professional musician and a professional printer in the sense that I belonged to both the musician's union and the printer's union. You had to take stiff tests to get into both organizations in those days. For the musician's union you were judged by a board of professional musicians, some of whom played in the St. Louis Symphony.

I was eighteen years old when I graduated from high school, and I knew then that my future was set. I had two loves, music and printing, and come what might, I would be making my living at one or the other for the rest of my life. At that time neither occupation demanded a college education, and I don't see how I could have afforded one anyway. Thus I looked forward to making my own way with my flute and my compositor's stick. I still had my dream of playing in a big theater orchestra like Mr. Sauter. It was time to be getting about making it come true.

11

T·W·O

FOR A WHILE after I graduated from high school I stayed in St. Louis working at the Rapid Printing Company and taking flute lessons from Mr. Sauter. My grandmother had come back from California, so I lived with her again. I also kept active in leading orchestras. We expanded the high school dance band and called it the White Rose Orchestra, because my grandmother thought White Rose was a pretty name. I also formed a fifteen-piece group to play classical music. For a time that unit rehearsed at my grandmother's house, all fifteen musicians somehow jamming themselves into my little room.

The trumpet player in my dance band was going with a girl named Florence Howell, and she had a sister named Leretta. I started dating Leretta to keep my friend company. It wasn't long until she and I were pretty serious about each other. Florence Howell was a good pianist, and she would come and play piano in the White Rose Orchestra so I could take Leretta out. Then on July 20, 1925, Leretta and I ran over to Belleville, Illinois, and got married. She was to remain my wife for forty-one years.

Leretta came from a musical family—she herself played the violin—who were also strong Baptists. Their church, the Third Baptist Church on Grand Street, had a good-sized orchestra, and when I started dating her, I began to take my flute over and play with that group. Soon one of the Sunday school classes there asked me to help them form an orchestra for them, so by then I was leading three musical aggregations at the same time.

Then I also began playing in a band at the Naval Reserve Station down on Ferry Street in St. Louis. The flute and piccolo that I owned were wooden, but I really wanted to play on good silver instruments. I became friendly with the concertmaster of the orchestra at the Missouri Theater who also played E-flat clarinet in the Naval Reserve Band on his night off from the movies. He told me the band needed a piccolo player and that if I would join, he was sure they would let me use their instruments, which were silver.

That was enough for me, so I joined that band, and it was through it that I was fortunate enough to have one of the most exciting experiences of my musical career. Now you have to remember that there were not too many musically trained flute players in St. Louis at this time and almost all of those who were, were playing almost every night in theater orchestras. Well, it happened that John Philip Sousa and his band were booked to play a one-week engagement at the Convention Hall and the band was short a flute player. Sousa decided to fill the spot with local talent, and of course, with his connections with the U.S. Navy the first place his manager looked was the Naval Reserve Band. I was available, so the leader of the Reserve Band contacted me and asked me if I wanted to try out.

You can imagine how I felt when I attended the rehearsal of that famous band before the first show. There were several other flute players there, so I didn't think I had much chance, but one of Sousa's baritone horn players kept encouraging me.

"Keep it up, young man," he would say, "and you'll be playing with us. If Mr. Sousa doesn't say anything to you when the rehearsal is over, you're in."

Mr. Sousa never did say anything, and I was able to play the whole week with the Sousa Band. Even though this was a relatively short time, many things about Mr. Sousa impressed themselves on my memory. Sousa was a strict, no-nonsense conductor. He didn't indulge in fancy theatrics on the podium, but he commanded so much respect that he had all the musi-

14

cians' attention all the time. He was a very religious man, and all of his band members had to follow a rigorous code of behavior. There was no smoking or drinking on the band, and none of the regular members could be married. This was because the band was constantly traveling, and Mr. Sousa thought the road was a bad environment for marriage.

Sousa had one trick that I still remember as clearly as if I had seen him do it yesterday. On his "Manhattan Beach" march the band would start the trio at double pianissimo and then build to a forte the first time through. Then as the last strain neared its end, Sousa would raise his baton high over his head and slowly bring it down. As that baton descended, the band got softer and softer until by the time it reached its lowest point the march was over and the music had faded entirely away. It was a tremendously impressive effect.

By the way, most of the marches in a Sousa concert were not listed on the program. The band would play a major work, and then Sousa would run a march in as an unannounced encore much in the way the Boston Pops Orchestra does even today in its concerts. At a Sousa concert, however, a stagehand would carry a large placard on stage presenting the name of the encore to the audience. These encores were always short; sometimes the band would play only second endings to the marches.

I don't make a lot out of my brief experience with Sousa. People think you're putting on a little if you say, "Well, I played with the Sousa Band," and I was never a regular member. But I still have a great deal of pride in the fact that I was good enough to be even a small part of that great organization for a short time. There was a thrill to playing under Sousa's baton that no amount of time can take away from me. John Philip Sousa was more than the March King; he was the King of Musicians.

In spite of all my musical activities I still had to keep working at the Rapid Printing Company to make a living. I liked the job, and after a while I was even able to buy myself a partnership in the firm, but I was still restless. I had never given up my dream of playing in a theater orchestra like Mr. Sauter. Now it seemed that the time might be drawing near when I could realize it. I talked the matter over with my teacher. He said he didn't think I was ready to play in the St. Louis theaters yet and advised me to get a copy of *Billboard* magazine.

"Just answer some of the ads for theater musicians in that," he said. "You can start out playing in some small town, and then when you've got some experience you can come back here to the city."

I got a copy of *Billboard*, but I soon found that most of the ads were for full orchestras rather than for single musicians. I still had this concert orchestra practicing in my room, so I talked it over with its members, and a number of them were as eager as I to begin playing in the movies. We cut our instrumentation down to seven pieces, about right for a reasonably sized theater orchestra, and started rehearsing movie music. I got hold of some theater cue sheets and a home movie projector, and we practiced right in my grandmother's living room.

Playing music for the silent movies was a demanding and highly specialized kind of work. Every theater had to have some kind of music to accompany the flickering images on the screen. The smallest ones had only pianos. Then a violin or a trumpet might be added. The next step up was a three-piece combo consisting of piano, trumpet, and drums. Next a clarinet player would be added, then a trombone, then a flute, then a cello, and then a string bass. In the large cities the really first-rate theaters might have orchestras of fifteen or twenty pieces. All of these units played not only for the films but also for the vaudeville acts that were often added to the program while the reels were being changed. Frequently the orchestras gave short concerts before the movies began.

Each theater manager would hire an orchestra leader to provide his music. The leader would usually have his own library of standard theater pieces. These had their own special names. "Hurries," for example, were fast numbers played behind action scenes in the films. "Mysteriosos" were mood pieces played to heighten the suspense, and so on. Some of these were especially written for the films; others were adaptations of existing works. Every film that came to the theater would be accompanied by a lead-sheet score that contained the various cues in the movie and the number to be played at each cue. For example, at a point in a picture when the cavalry was to charge the lead sheet might look something like this:

> (Cue) . . . Let's charge!
> Gallop from *William Tell* Overture
> Gallop from *Light Cavalry* Overture

The second, and sometimes third, numbers listed were alternatives in case the leader did not have the first one. If he had none of the listed numbers, he at least knew the type of music required and could make his own substitutions.

Most pictures also came with some original themes written especially for that movie, just as original music is written for pictures today. These were coded by color. Whenever, a red card popped up in a player's music, for example, he knew to cut immediately to the "red theme," which was usually the opening theme for the picture. When a blue card appeared, he cut to the "blue theme," and so on.

Really big movies were accompanied by complete scores for fifteen-piece orchestra. I still have a couple of these scores, one for D. W. Griffith's *Orphans of the Storm* and one for *The Ten Commandments* directed by Cecil B. deMille. These scores resemble those of Broadway musicals today. Each part is carefully bound in paper; the conductor's part is a thick book with each cue marked at the start of each page. Usually these cues are the lines that were flashed on the screen between the action frames, but sometimes they are bits of business in the action itself. For example:

> (Start at . . . "I'm leaving now.")

and

> (Start when horses and chariots enter.)

Many of the smaller movie houses would augment their orchestras especially to play for these big movies.

Of course, all the music had to be carefully synchronized with the action of the picture. A theater musician had to be constantly on the alert to change from one piece to another,

17

for starting and stopping depended on not the music but the action on the screen. These rapid changes were facilitated by a system of lights. A red light was attached to each music stand and wired to a push button on the director's stand. When the director reached a cue to change numbers, he would push his button and the lights on the stands would come on signaling the players to cut to the next piece. It took considerable discipline to watch the music, the conductor, and the red light all at the same time. And usually the theater musician was lucky if there was one rehearsal before the orchestra played for the first matinee. Good sight-reading was essential for a theater player.

I rehearsed my orchestra extensively for a few weeks, and then we began answering the ads in *Billboard*. Nothing much materialized until I got a nibble from a gentleman, whose name I can't remember, in Selma, Alabama. He wanted me to lead an orchestra in a place he called the Academy of Music. This didn't sound much like a movie theater, but this fellow was talking about a steady, six-day-a-week job, and in those days steady work was hard to find. Finally, I agreed that I would go down to Selma, taking with me my music library and one of my brothers-in-law, Ray Howell, who played trombone. I was to go down first, because Ray had a job with the railroad in St. Louis, and he felt he should give a couple of days' notices.

Thus it was that one day in the spring of 1925 I boarded the train to Selma with a big box of music under my arm. I still didn't have the foggiest notion of what the Academy of Music might be, but during the two-day ride I happened to meet a woman from Selma who told me that it was a big movie theater. Here I had given up hope of a theater job only to find that that was exactly where I was going to work!

When I got off the train in Selma the stationmaster told me that the manager of the theater would send someone for my luggage. He pointed me the way to the Academy of Music, which was only three blocks from the station, and I walked to it. It was a lovely Saturday evening, and I could see right away that Selma was one of the most beautiful cities I had ever been in. It was very southern with gracious old houses and wide,

18

clean streets. It was also very southern in another way in that it was very segregated. Black people would get off the sidewalk when they met a white person, and they would stop their wagons and cars whenever a white person started to cross the street, whether it was at a corner or in the middle of the block.

The theater manager greeted me warmly and wanted me to start playing as soon as possible, but there appeared to be a lack of musicians for the orchestra.

"We can get some players from the union here and in Montgomery," the manager told me, "and you say your brother-in-law will be coming in a day or so. I've got a drummer for you already. I don't think he reads music very well, but I guess he'll be all right."

If he doesn't read music, he's not going to be all right, I thought to myself, but I said nothing.

"Oh, and I can get you a real good trumpet player," the manager went on. "He's Vincent Lopez's brother. He's first rate. Of course, he just had all his teeth pulled."

By this time I was pretty sure I was going to have a few problems, but there was nothing to do right then but go along with the manager. There happened to be a rooming house almost next door to the theater, so I got a room there. Then I had dinner and spent the rest of the evening watching the picture at the theater to get an idea of the kind of music I would need for it.

The next morning I set about lining up musicians, and with the help of the union I managed to scrounge up an orchestra in time to play for the next matinee. Joe Lopez turned out to be as good as advertised even without teeth, and he was a big help to me. You have to remember that I was only twenty years at that time, and this was my first job. I was really a "first of May," as they used to call greenhorns in the music business. I don't remember if we used the nonreading drummer or not, but somebody played drums that afternoon.

Then in a couple of days my brother-in-law Ray came. He got in on the evening train, and the theater manager had him go right to the pit to play the night show.

"Ted's new and a little nervous," he told Ray. "I think he'll feel a lot better once you're there."

So right in the middle of the night show I looked up and there was Ray blowing trombone, and the manager was right, I did feel a lot better.

We quickly settled into the routine of playing for the movies six days a week. Like most large movie houses at that time the Academy of Music also featured vaudeville acts mixed in with the films. I sometimes had problems with the vaudeville performers, because some of them were very demanding about their music, and I was so young, but usually the manager backed me up if I couldn't handle the situation myself. I remember one visiting singer who called himself Joyful George and had quite a reputation at that time, coming to me complaining about the theater orchestra in Montgomery, his last stop.

"One of my big numbers is 'Melody in F,' " he said, "but I've decided it would sound better if I sang it in E-flat. Can your boys put it down a tone? That damned orchestra in Montgomery couldn't transpose it."

I told him we could make the transposition, but it was going to be a little strange playing "Melody in F" in E-flat. He insisted, nevertheless, so we rehearsed, and although it didn't sound very good, Joyful George was happy. Still I wasn't satisfied. I knew the song would sound a lot better in the key in which it was originally written.

I talked the matter over with Joe Lopez before the matinee.

"Hell," he said, "play the thing in F if you want to. That S.O.B. hasn't got an ear good enough to tell the difference anyway."

That night, with some trepidation, I led the orchestra through "Melody in F" in its intended key while Joyful George sang his heart out. Joe was right. He never knew the difference. He got a big hand, and after the show he came down to the pit raving about my orchestra that could play a song in any key.

I played the entire 1925 season at the Academy of Music, but it was not all smooth sailing. The trouble was the manager did not really know just what he wanted in music. He was constantly interfering in the selections I made to accompany the films. The score would call for a certain number, and I'd have it and be ready to play it, but the manager would decide that I should play a popular medley instead, because he thought the young people liked jazz. This wouldn't really fit with the action on the screen, and the people would complain. At the end of the season I gave him my notice, and Ray and I and some others went back to St. Louis. The Selma adventure had been good experience and convinced me that leading, or at least playing in, a theater orchestra was the thing I wanted to do in life. I now intended to look around to find a better situation in which to do it.

T·H·R·E·E

BACK IN ST. LOUIS I started working some
at the printing company again and rehearsing my orchestra at
my grandmother's house. Once again we poured over every
copy of *Billboard* and sent out letters. It wasn't long before I
got two prospects almost at the same time. One was for me
alone. A Mr. Woods in Columbia, Missouri, wanted me to play
flute in an orchestra that he was forming for a theater he was
about to open there. The other offer was from a doctor in
Monroe, South Carolina, who wanted my entire orchestra.
The South Carolina job sounded more exciting, so I wrote
back to the doctor and we worked out the details.

That job really sounded like something. The doctor
wanted us to play not only in his movie theater but also in a
dance hall he owned and for other social events. Our
employer was waiting at the station when my six musicians
and I got off the train, and we had hardly got our luggage off
the baggage car when he hustled us down to his dance hall to
play. After that, however, we got a series of unpleasant
shocks.

The first came at the dance. The doctor had told us that
the crowd there went exclusively for old-time music — polkas,
waltzes, and schottisches. We played one set of polkas, and
absolutely nobody danced, nor did they dance to the waltzes

and schottisches we played after that. Finally, a few young people came up to the stand.

"Can't you guys play anything but that corny, old-time stuff?" one of them asked me.

"But Doctor Stewart said that you liked the old-time numbers," I said.

"Oh, you can't pay any attention to Doctor Stewart," the young fellow said. "He got shell-shocked in the war. You can't believe a word he says."

Seven musicians exchanged worried looks.

Fortunately we had enough popular numbers in our library to satisfy the crowd, but after the dance the full extent of our misfortune began to become known to us. The doctor's great theater turned out to be a bandbox that could hardly accommodate a piano let alone a seven-piece orchestra. The rest of his promises turned out to be just about as realistic. By the afternoon of the next day it had become clear that there simply was not enough work to support a seven-piece orchestra in Monroe, South Carolina. It was also plain that there was not enough money among the seven of us to get us all back to St. Louis. We were stuck.

We hung around Monroe all that day and then went down to the railroad station that evening to meet a fellow who was going to play saxophone with us but had been unable to make the trip with the rest of us. He had more experience than we and had spent quite a bit of time on the road before.

"That doctor can't do this to us," he said positively. "He's got us down here under false pretenses. We can have the union on him and maybe sue him for breach of contract or something besides. Let's give him a call. The least he can do is give us train fare back to St. Louis. There's a train leaving at midnight. We're going to be on it."

We called the doctor and told him we wanted to go back to St. Louis. He was astonished that we wanted to leave and launched into another long spiel about how he was going to build us a fancy conservatory and I don't know what all, but we weren't buying. Finally he said he would take care of us. Now he may have been shell-shocked, but his family was well-to-do, and he had enough pull to get a banker to come in and open up the bank at ten o'clock that night. He gave us not only enough money for the train tickets but an extra fifty dollars apiece, and that was big money in those days. Still it was a long ride back to St. Louis. Here we had started off with high hopes of a more or less permanent, high-paying job, and now two days later here we were back, eight musicians still out of work.

I thought it over while the miles clicked away beneath the wheels and decided that I had had enough of orchestra leading. As soon as I got off the train in St. Louis I wired Mr. Woods, the fellow in Columbia, Missouri, that I would take the job of flutist that he had offered me. A wire came back almost immediately. "Sorry, position filled." I had lost out all the way around.

Well, you can imagine how I felt then. That night I was sitting on the back porch of my mother-in-law's house with a friend trying to forget my troubles when along came another Western Union messenger with another telegram for me from Mr. Woods.

"Can use you immediately in a smaller orchestra in a smaller theater, stop. Must come immediately."

I let out a whoop, and my friend and I started right then for the Western Union station even though it meant walking several blocks and then taking a streetcar. I wired back that I accepted the position and caught the midnight bus for Columbia. I don't think Leretta had even had a chance to unpack my trunk from the Monroe fiasco.

This job turned out to be on the level. Mr. Woods managed all three theaters in Columbia, and I played in a seven-piece orchestra in the Hall Theater, which was owned by Mr. Woods' father-in-law, Mr. Hall. The group was led by an elderly man named Jack Whitney whose wife played piano for us. The Whitneys had been troopers on the vaudeville and circus circuits and were both excellent musicians.

I brought Leretta to Columbia, and we settled down in an apartment across the street from Christian College. I got thirty-five dollars a week playing matinees and evening shows six nights a week. These were good wages in those days. I could buy enough groceries for five dollars to carry Leretta and me, and later our daughter, for a week. In fact, on Sundays when there was no movie our whole orchestra would sometimes pile into a couple of cars and drive to Jefferson City to kid the orchestras who played in the theaters there. They had to play on Sundays, and they got no more money than we did.

I learned a lot about music in Columbia. The theater orchestras in those days were very close-knit groups, almost like families. I learned about the various instruments from listening to my fellow musicians talk about their problems, which they invariably did on breaks. I learned to play saxophone, because the theater manager wanted us woodwind players to double on sax. The saxophone was just becoming popular, and to play modern dance music orchestras really had to have them. At first, if you doubled on another instrument, you got paid time and a half. The theaters just couldn't afford to pay that extra money, though, so finally the union dropped that regulation, and you got no more extra money if you doubled.

Theater playing was demanding work. A typical movie program in 1926 would consist of the news, a one-reel comedy, a cartoon, and the main feature. The orchestra played for all of these, but it usually had a break midway in the feature for about five minutes. In the smaller theaters they would just keep on showing the film without music; in the larger ones a piano or organ would play. The Hall Theater had no organ, because Mr. Woods, who was a bass player, didn't like organs.

On Saturdays we had vaudeville acts to play for. In some respects these were harder to play than the movies, because each act had its own special music and we had the same problems that I had encountered in Selma. Sometimes we just played marches to cover the vaudeville acts. We would start out playing a march very softly with the curtain closed. Then we would repeat it very loudly, the curtain would open, and the act would come on. This helped to get the audience excited and responsive to what was to come once the performers appeared.

In spite of our busy schedule, there was always time for fun and kidding around. Our director's wife, Mrs. Whitney, was often the ringleader in practical jokes. Since I was the youngest member of the orchestra, she liked to single me out especially. Often the vaudeville acts would feature a girl singer or a troop of dancing girls. Mrs. Whitney would sometimes corner a singer and tell her, "Look, the flute player there is the youngest and best-looking fellow in the orchestra. Why don't you sing a song especially for him, or throw him a rose when you finish or something?" Mrs. Whitney knew that my wife would always be in the audience. The girl would make over me, Leretta would get jealous and give me the dickens, and of course, I wouldn't know what was going on.

One time one of Mrs. Whitney's tricks almost backfired. She got me into a game of Mah-Jongg with an all-girl dance troop when I didn't know that Leretta was waiting for me out in front. As I said, a theater orchestra in those days was a lot like a big family. Every Friday the wives of the musicians would get together and prepare a big spaghetti dinner or some other big feed for us all to share after the evening show. On the day of the card game Leretta had five fresh-baked pies for the evening dinner cooling while she went to the matinee. She was so furious when she found out about the card game that she went right home and threw every one of those pies into the garbage. Then she came back and lit into me.

Mrs. Whitney saw that she had gone too far, so she stepped in and explained to Leretta how she had set up the whole thing. Then it was Leretta's turn to feel bad. During the evening show she got someone to mind our baby while she sneaked home and baked up five more pies. Thus we had our usual dessert after all, but Leretta had enough of baking by the time the day was over.

Some of the jokes were more musical. In one number I had a flute cadenza that I really liked to play. This cadenza finished in a little downward arpeggio that ended on a low C. I was very proud of my low C, because I could bring it out with a nice full tone almost like that of a cello. One day Mrs. Whitney got the fellow sitting next to me to run a slip of paper up the inside of my flute until it just blocked the low-C hole. I came gliding down in my arpeggio, and when I reached the arpeggio absolutely no sound came out. The harder I blew, the more silence I got. Of course, I was terribly embarrassed, but everybody else was breaking up.

Another time I made the mistake of boasting to the others how fond I was of Limburger cheese and onion sandwiches, a fact of which they were already painfully aware. The next day

I opened my flute case to find Limburger cheese smeared all over my mouthpiece. It took me a week to be able to pucker up to blow without wrinkling my nose at the same time.

All in all, it was a good life, and I might still be playing at the Hall Theater had it not been for a picture that came out in 1927 called *The Jazz Singer* staring Al Jolson. It was the first talking movie, and in a few months the handwriting was on the wall as far as theater orchestras were concerned. As soon as the sound started coming along with the film there was no need for a pit orchestra. We movie musicians would soon be as extinct as the dodo.

We didn't lose our jobs overnight, of course. Mr. Woods and Mr. Hall were good men, and they kept us as long as they could. At first only a few of the bigger pictures had sound, and even after most of the features were talkies there were still the cartoons, the comedies, and the news to play for. For a while some of the theaters even advertised "live music" as a publicity device. But the opportunities to play gradually became fewer and fewer, and one by one the theater orchestras folded up shop.

In the Hall orchestra we knew our days were numbered. The cornetist in our group was Frank Flack who became a very dear friend of mine. Frank, whose real name was Michael Corino—he had been adopted by the Flack family—was a thoroughly trained musician, having directed a navy band on a ship during World War I.

"Ted," he would say to me, "these talking pictures are going to come, and we're going to be out of a job. Now I'll tell you what we'll do. We'll go to some small town around here, and we'll start an orchestra. The biggest churches in most towns are the Methodist and the Baptist. I've been a Methodist all my life, and you can join the Baptist church. We'll get those churches behind us, and that's the way we'll get our orchestra going."

Maybe that sounds a little strange, but that was the kind of thinking that theater musicians were doing in those days, and a lot of them did go into directing and teaching. Maybe it's not such a coincidence that the public school band movement began just a few years after talking pictures ended theater orchestras.

28

Anyway, Frank Flack helped me enormously by teaching me conducting and the rudiments of playing brass instruments. After our usual Friday postshow dinners we'd go up to his room, and he'd work with me. Of course, I already played flute and saxophone and I knew the rudiments of the clarinet, so with Frank's help I got a pretty extensive knowledge of band instruments. I had also picked up a lot about string playing just from listening to the violin players discussing their parts during our breaks in the movies. Thus by the time Mr. Hall had to let us go I thought I might be able to go into music teaching if I had to, even though I didn't join in Frank's town band scheme.

The ax finally fell in late 1928, and Leretta and I took our little daughter and moved back to St. Louis. Many theaters in the big city still had orchestras, sometimes just to play concerts before the movies, and I felt my opportunities would be better there. It was rough going, however. Musicians were scrambling for work, and to make matters worse the musicians' union entered into a long strike. For months a union musician couldn't play at all.

We had to live somehow, so I fell back on my other great love and opened a printing shop. I rented a little place on Union Avenue not far from the big General Motors automobile plant, and for a while we did fairly well, because we got a lot of orders from the plant. Leretta helped me with the bookwork, and I was able to hire one other fellow to aid with the printing. But I wasn't ready to give up my music by any means. I kept practicing my flute, taking some more lessons from Mr. Sauter, and kept hoping.

Then one afternoon when I was busy setting up an advertising flyer I got a call from Maurice Barnet, the manager of the Pageant Theater, offering me a job playing flute and saxophone there. That was the way I found out the musicians' strike had ended. I got pretty excited. The Pageant Theater was part of the largest theater chain in St. Louis. It was owned by three Greek brothers named Skouras.

I was part of a sixteen-piece orchestra at the Pageant. The Skouras brothers never stinted on music. But we did a lot more than just play for the pictures. Since so many of the films were now talkies the orchestra had to become a show in itself, and one of the provisions in the new union contract was that musicians could, "become actors." Thus, in breaks in the pictures we members of the orchestra would do skits and routines. At that time, for example, the tune "Singing in the Rain" was popular. They dressed me up in my wife's fur coat and gave me a sprinkling can. While one of the saxophone players sang "Singing in the Rain," I stood on a step ladder with a sign, "Vesuvius," around my neck and poured real water on him. Maybe it sounds corny today, but that's the kind of thing theater orchestras did to stay in business in 1928.

I played in the Pageant Theater orchestra for about a year and kept the printing shop going in the mornings, because I knew how chancy theater playing was becoming. Then even the Skouras brothers had to admit that talkies were here to stay, and I was back to scrambling for musical jobs again. I answered an ad in *Billboard* for a job in Kansas City and drove all the way there only to find that it was a fake. I remember that very clearly, because I had eleven flat tires on my old Chevrolet coming back. Then I picked up a little work subing for a saxophone player at the dog track in St. Louis, but those were rough times. It was early 1930, and the full force of the Great Depression was just hitting. I was a long way from being the only person looking for work.

Finally, I saw an ad in *Billboard* for a job in a repertory theater company headed by a man named Harley Sadler. I already knew something about Sadler from Jack Whitney of the Hall Theater orchestra who had told me that he was an honest man and easy to work for, so I answered the ad and he sent me fifty dollars to come join him and his show in Clovis, New Mexico. When I got off the train in Clovis, however, there was no Harley and no show. The whole enterprise had moved on, so it was back on the train until I finally caught up with my new employer at the great metropolis of Mule Shoe, Texas.

Even though I only worked for Sadler for a few weeks, I enjoyed the experience. We had a fifteen-piece band with most of us doubling, and we provided all the music for the various vaudeville and dramatic presentations that made up the company's repertoire. The show would come to a town under the auspices of the American Legion or one of the churches, and our performances were held in a big circus tent. Sometimes the band would march in a parade in the morning before the show to drum up business. Then before the performance started we would play marches and waltzes out in front of the tent. Harley Sadler was a very religious man, and he would sometimes hold prayer meetings before the performances. Before he hired me he inquired carefully into my morals and religious beliefs.

Well, it was not a bad job, but I was a long way from home, and naturally I missed Leretta, my daughter, Bea, and my new son, Teddy. Traveling with a tent show was hardly the kind of life for them, so I wasn't completely happy. I also still had the printing shop back in St. Louis. Luckily, another music job opened up closer to home almost immediately. Even though I could hardly imagine it at that time, this new job was to prove a little more lasting than any I had had before. In fact, over fifty years later I guess in a way I'm still at it.

F·O·U·R

AT ABOUT THE time I had answered Harley Sadler's ad in *Billboard* I had noticed another ad in that magazine:

> Wanted: Professional musician familiar with all instruments to establish youth band in West Frankfort, Illinois. Applicants should contact Sherman Alemanrode, Manager, C. G. Conn Musical Instrument Co.

A St. Louis address was listed. I had filled out an application for this job, although since I had no formal training on any instruments except flute and piano, I didn't think I had much chance of getting it. I didn't hear anything more, so when Sadler's offer came, I naturally took that.

I had been with Sadler about two weeks—we were still in Mule Shoe, Texas—when a wire came from Leretta. The West Frankfort job was mine if I wanted it. Did I want to come back to St. Louis? I thought it over a little and then told Sadler I was leaving. He was decent about it and told me that if the West Frankfort job didn't work out, I could come back and work for him. I caught the first train back north.

In accepting the position with the Conn Company I was taking a job very much like that of Professor Harold Hill in

Meredith Willson's *Music Man*, except that it was on the level. The Conn Company was the largest manufacturer of musical instruments in the world. Its home base was, and still is, Elkhart, Indiana, but it had branches throughout the country. At that time it promoted its instruments by sending salesmen into small towns who would get up big meetings to rent instruments to boys and girls with the understanding that the company would provide a teacher for a month to get them started. At the end of that time those children who wanted to continue would buy the instruments. The company teachers got a small salary and a commission on every instrument they sold when the month was over.

I got into St. Louis late on Tuesday, September 17, 1930. Leretta told me that Sherman Alemanrode expected me to leave for West Frankfort with him early the next morning. I wasn't even too sure exactly where West Frankfort, Illinois, was, but somehow Leretta got my suitcase repacked, and I struggled down to the Conn Company early Wednesday morning. There was Alemanrode waiting for me with an enormous Page limousine. He looked even worse than I felt. He told me that he had been out partying with some friends the night before, and the effects were still evident.

Somehow Mr. Alemanrode herded that Page across the Popular Street Bridge, but almost as soon as we got out of East St. Louis he pulled over to the side of the road.

"Ted," he said, "I've just got to get a nap, or I'm not going to live through the day. You drive. Just follow this route here on the map."

Well, I'd spent a lot of time behind the wheel, but it had been the wheel of my Chevy coup. I wasn't sure I could handle a tank like the Page, but you don't argue with your boss when you've only been on the job fifteen minutes. I got behind the wheel, and Alemanrode climbed into the backseat and went to sleep. Somehow I kept everything on my side of the road until we got to West Frankfort. I must have made quite an appearance my first time in town rolling down Main Street behind the wheel of that huge Page.

When I first came to West Frankfort it was a town of about nineteen thousand located a hundred miles southeast of St. Louis and about seventy miles northwest of Paducah, Kentucky. Most of the town stretches out along an unusually long main street that runs east and west and is actually Illinois Highway 149. Basically, it was a farm and mining town servicing the two major industries of southern Illinois. West Frankfort is in the heart of the Illinois coal-mining district, and as the mines go so goes the town. This is also just about at the break between the farmlands of the upper midwest and the hilly, wooded country of the south. North of West Frankfort the crops are corn, soybeans, and oats. South of it are peach and apple orchards.

West Frankfort was originally simply Frankfort. The town began on a hill east of the present location in an area now known as Frankfort Heights. When the railroad came through, the town moved west to meet it, and hence the name, West Frankfort.

It was a booming place in the fall of 1930 in spite of the Great Depression. The mines were going full blast, and work was around the clock. The miners worked in three shifts, so large groups of them would be getting off work at all kinds of odd hours. These men would come up tired and hungry and would look for some place to eat, so there were restaurants scattered up and down Main Street that were open almost twenty-four hours a day. There were few autos then, but you could go down Main Street just about any time of day or night and find groups of people walking up and down. Later, after Leretta joined me, we would often go back to St. Louis for a visit. Sometimes we would leave the city around midnight when the night spots were closing down, and we'd say to each other, "Well, things should just about be getting started in West Frankfort."

That Wednesday in 1930 Sherman Alemanrode and I reached town in the middle of the afternoon. Sherman woke up and got into the front seat with me. He told me to go directly to the high school, which was easy to find because it was just where it is today, right on Main Street. In the high school auditorium we met Mr. Olie Maire who was the Conn salesman for the district and had brought the instruments. Olie was a fine saxophonist in his own right and later would often play solos with my West Frankfort bands. That day we shook hands as the auditorium began to fill up with grade-school children who had been let out a little early expressly to get their instruments. Soon we had a hall full of eight- to twelve-year-olds goggling at all those horns that Maire had displayed on the stage.

When all the children had assembled, Alemanrode and Maire handed out the instruments. As each child received his, I took him aside and showed him how to put it together without damaging it terminally before we could have our first lesson. This was especially important with the clarinets, which were all metal. In those days beginners' clarinets were usually made of metal, and even the clarinetists in the United States Navy Band used metal instruments. These clarinets came in two parts, and there was what was called a "bridge key" that could be jammed if they were put together in a ham-fisted manner.

For a ten-dollar rental fee each child got a month's use of his instrument, lessons, a lesson book, and, if I remember correctly, even a wire music stand. Then if the child decided to buy the horn at the end of the month, seven dollars of the fee went against the price of the instrument. The Conn Company put out two lines of instruments at that time, the relatively high-priced Conn line and an economy line under the name of Pan American. The horns we gave out were all Pan American. The process took a long time, because we had seventy-four children waiting there. I was expected to teach each one of them to play well enough to be able to put on a concert in just one month.

Finally, the last child had gone off with his new treasure, and Mr. Alemanrode and Mr. Maire then got around to registering me at the local hotel, the Demmick, like almost everything else in West Frankfort, right on Main Street. I stayed there three nights, and then Olie Maire directed me to a rooming house run by a Mrs. Ida Barrett where I got room and board at a very reasonable price. It was right across the street north from what was then called the Central School and only about three blocks from the high school. Then Olie Maire left to go to another town. Sherman Alemanrode had already returned to St. Louis. I was on my own.

I plunged into working with the children. Obviously, I couldn't see each of these students individually enough to get him ready to play the concert, so I had to use a class instruction

36

method, which was relatively new in those days. The only class method book then available was *The Bennett Band Book,* which I found out years later was written by Henry Fillmore. This was the instruction book the children got with their instruments, and it was a godsend to me.

Fortunately, I had the complete cooperation of the superintendent of schools, Mr. C. A. Waller, a real gentleman and a cultured and educated person. He allowed me to use the grade school building after classes and at night for my lessons, and I was even able to teach some of the children during school hours when they had study periods. The other schoolteachers were very supportive, also, even though I had absolutely no formal connection with the school system. But this was something that the town wanted. I found out later that the whole grade school band idea had started when a group of parents had gone to Superintendent Waller and the school board and asked them to contact the Conn Company.

You see, in those days most of the Illinois miners were recent emigrants from Europe, especially eastern Europe. Life in the mines is not easy even today, but in the thirties modern mechanization and safety standards were almost entirely lacking, and the miners had a very tough time. But they all had a dream that someday their children would be better off than they and not have to sweat for low wages underground. Music, they thought, might be one way for them to make this dream come true.

I can still remember many times after I had established the West Frankfort music program when some huge miner, his pores still full of coal dust, would come up to me with a grimy little child in one hand and a clarinet or a trumpet case in the other and say, "You make him work. He no work, you beat helly. Maybe some day he be big musician. Not have to work in mines like me."

For these people music could be the golden key that would unlock all the promise that America had originally held out to them in Romania or Hungary or some other place far across an ocean from West Frankfort.

Not that everyone was on my side. When the Conn Company came in and rented all those instruments, there were some businessmen in West Frankfort who got a little miffed that they hadn't thought of the idea first. After all, why should people in St. Louis and Indiana be raking in that profit in a time when local businesses were struggling to survive a depression? Southern Illinois folk are pretty insular, and they tend to distrust "foreigners," especially young whippersnappers from big cities. Remember, I was only twenty-five years old. And then there were some miners who just thought my task was impossible. "You no teach little kid to play horn. Take big, strong man to blow that thing."

Thus as the month passed, the odds around town began running about two to one that the coming grade school band concert was going to turn out to be a resounding flop. In fact, I found out later that one night a group of businessmen held a meeting in which it was hinted that, like Professor Harold Hill, I was a phony who would pocket all the instrument rental money and run. These worries were partly quieted by the fact that I had brought Leretta and my two children to town and my daughter was enrolled in school, but still the consensus was that I would bear close watching. It was also suggested that the coming concert had better be a success, or one music teacher just might find himself ridden out of town on a rail.

Although I wasn't aware of that meeting, one didn't have to be psychic to understand just how important that concert was going to be. As I drilled my students on the fundamentals I gave it a great deal of thought. West Frankfort obviously wasn't going to get a Sousa Band concert. Most of my students had no musical background whatsoever, so I was really starting from scratch. In addition, I had instrumentation problems. While the formation of a band was a good selling gimmick for the Conn Company, the firm was more interested in pushing horns than in contributing to the culture of a town. Thus, good old Olie had blessed me with no less than twenty-two alto saxophones and no drums!

With about a week to go, the concert gradually began to take shape in my mind. I settled on a few easy little numbers from *The Bennett Band Book,* and we practiced extensively on them. Sherman Alemanrode was going to come down from St. Louis and give a pep talk on the value of music and why all the children should go on and buy their horns, and I also arranged to have a couple of professional soloists from the big city to perform. West Frankfort already had a high school band of sorts, about eighteen pieces directed by a Miss Sorg who also taught vocal music on a part-time basis. The high school drummer had a trap set, and he agreed to come and fill our needs for a rhythm section.

Then I had an inspiration. I took two Stephen Foster songs, "Old Folks at Home" and "Old Black Joe," and arranged them in easy four-part harmony. I took my eight best saxophonists and divided them up on the parts forming a kind of double-sax quartet. They would be the feature attraction. If I had twenty-two saxophones, I reasoned, I might just as well make use of them.

We drilled literally night and day, and by the evening of the concert I felt we had a fighting chance of making a presentable performance. The *West Frankfort American*, the local paper did two stories on the band during the final week before the concert. The second one concluded with an interview with me quoted at length. I praised the children, the school, the administrators, and everyone else I could think of—legitimately, because they had all been great—and told the reporter: "It has been my pleasure to instruct many a band in various parts of these United States, but never before have I had such a large percentage to make good in a single group of seventy or more students as in this community of West Frankfort." Well, at least the part about never having had such a large percentage make good was the truth.

Finally, Monday, October 20, 1930, came. The high school auditorium, which held a thousand people, began filling up as early as six-thirty that evening, and by eight o'clock there wasn't even standing room in that hall. About half of the audience was made up of parents and others who were hoping to be impressed by the musical ability of the children. The other half came to witness the flop they had been predicting. Their attitude was not very different from that of people who go to auto races hoping for an accident. I got the band tuned, spoke a few words that I hoped were reassuring to the children, and the curtain went up.

What happened after that was described by the *West Frankfort American* reporter under the headline, "Great Concert by School Band Here Last Night:"

> That music has its charm was spendidly shown last night in the demonstration concert given by the school band to a capacity audience in the high school auditorium. . . . The band has been organized four weeks under the competent direction of T. W. Paschedag during the period of its organization and what that man has been able to develop in a musical way with the band members is almost unbelievable.
>
> When the curtain arose on that scene of the seventy-one members in instrumentation formation there was a burst of applause from that great audience that gave evidence of their appreciation of this great work.
>
> There stood the director hands raised as a signal for readiness, and as his hands came down there was a burst of music that thrilled the audience, for the assembly was spellbound as they listened to the rendition of the program presented by these juvenile performers, for it had a charm far beyond the most sanguine expectation.

Not a bad write-up for "Abide with Me" and "Lightly Row," eh? Actually, the children did very, very well, and after the first number even the skeptics were applauding enthusiastically. And when my eight saxophones came out front and launched into "Old Folks at Home," those people just went wild. They'd never heard anything like eight saxes playing together before—maybe nobody has ever heard it since, either. By the time Sherman Alemanrode gave his talk, the audience was completely sold on the grade school band idea. So impressed were they with the children that the soloists from St. Louis—who undoubtedly deserved to have been the high point of the concert—went virtually ignored. The *American* reporter didn't even take the trouble to mention their names in his story.

The evening was especially gratifying to me, because despite what I had told the *American* I was hardly a music educator. I'd had one lone flute student for a while in St. Louis, but I was nothing more or less than a professional musician. But during that hectic month of preparing for the concert I'd discovered that I enjoyed working with children and seeing them respond and develop as musicians. Leretta and I had come to like West Frankfort and the many fine people who had worked so hard to help us. It was good to justify their confidence and to prove to the skeptics that I wasn't a phony, that in spite of my lack of experience and my twenty-two saxophones I could get the job done.

But now the concert was over, and that was supposed to be that. I was going to turn the band over to Miss Sorg at the high school and move on. To what I wasn't very sure. A few nights later, however, a group of band parents asked me to come to a meeting they were holding at the American Legion Hall in town. It was a put-up job, because the meeting was actually a reception for Leretta and me, but we did talk some business in the course of the evening. The parents told me that they hated to see me go now that the band was off to such a good start. Might the Conn Company be persuaded to let me stay on another month just to solidify things a bit? I said I didn't know, but I would see what I could do.

I talked it over with Sherman Alemanrode. He wrote some letters and made some calls, and in a couple of days the answer came. Yes, Conn would pay my salary for another month to stay in West Frankfort. I think part of the company's willingness might have been because we had such a high percentage of students who stayed in the band after the first month. Only about a dozen of the original group decided to drop out.

So then in addition to rehearsing the band and working with the children privately I got another chore to attend to. Sherman Alemanrode and I started calling on all the parents whose children were in the band. I'd haul out my grade book and show ma and pa how well little Johnny or Susie was doing, and then Sherman would make his pitch for Conn. The company really did offer easy terms—it had to because this was the very low point of the Great Depression—and almost every time the parents would somehow find that they could scratch up enough for a down payment. Often one of them would disappear for a little and come back with the money in a musty purse dug out of some secret hiding place or even exhumed from the backyard. Many of these miners and country folk didn't trust the banks, and with good reason, since so many of them had failed.

The second month passed, and then it looked as if my stay in West Frankfort really was going to come to an end. Even the Conn Company wasn't going to pay me to hang around any longer. But then in the middle of November a group of band parents and members of the American Legion Ladies Auxiliary paid a call on me. They told me they would like to have me stay as a teacher permanently. If they could guarantee enough private pupils for me to make a living, would I be interested? I talked it over with Leretta for a little, but there really wasn't much to talk about. We had fallen in love with West Frankfort in the two months we had spent there, and no other steady work seemed to be at hand. The next time the group met I told them I would be delighted to stay on the basis they suggested. By the time my second month came to an end I had enough private students signed up. Almost without my realizing it, my days as a wandering musician had ended. From then on I was the music man in West Frankfort.

F·I·V·E

T HE SUCCESS OF that first little concert had won me a job and awakened a good deal of interest in West Frankfort, but I knew that there was a lot of work to do to get a sound instrumental music program going. Since I was not officially connected with the public school system, most of the lessons I gave had to be offered after school and on weekends. I had over sixty pupils, so sometimes those lessons went on until eleven or twelve at night. In addition I formed my pupils into a private school band, and we had band rehearsal every Saturday morning. Because of the continuing enthusiasm among the school administrators we were allowed to rehearse this band in the Central School. Our practice room was in the basement and also happened to be the boys' restroom. For a while boys used the facilities in full view of the band while we played. Then one of the mothers saw her daughter playing flute under those conditions and went to the school board. They kindly installed a screen. The teachers also continued the practice of letting me give some lessons in the schools during study halls.

My grade school band was a lot of extra work, but I thought it was one of the most important things I did, because it kept the community involved in the music program. I knew that if these parents were going to hand over part of what little money they earned for music lessons for their children, they would have to be excited about music. Listening to little Johnny or Susie practicing scales and blowing wrong notes wasn't going to instill this excitement. My fathers and mothers wanted to hear real music from a band. Thus I formed a band for them, and it wasn't long until the people of West Frankfort began to think of it as their band and it was something they could be proud of. In those days music wasn't just a class in school or a lesson on Saturday. It was a community activity, and there were many times when we had almost as many parents and relatives at band rehearsals as we did musicians. They came to listen and enjoy because they were proud to watch their children develop, and besides, it was free. Any activity that was free drew large crowds in the Great Depression.

So all that year the band rehearsed and played. And did we play! We played for everything. We played concerts in the bandstand on Main Street, we played for the opening of an amusement house, we played for baseball games, we played at church picnics and union outings. Someone once said, a bit inelegantly, that you couldn't let a fart on Main Street without the West Frankfort Grade School Band showing up to blow it away. And the more we played, the more the community supported us. I often think that part of the problem with our school bands today is that they don't play enough concerts to entertain the public. Our bands play for the football and basketball games, and then maybe one or two concerts the rest of the year that only the band parents hear about. A community is not going to support a band if it doesn't even realize that it's around.

In spite of all this support, however, Leretta and I had a tough time financially. Fortunately, I soon found some ways to supplement my income. A drummer named Woosely headed a nine-piece dance orchestra out of Mt. Vernon, Illinois, about thirty miles north of West Frankfort, and I got a job playing sax for him. I also worked out an arrangement with my landlady, Mrs. Barrett, so that we could get our room and part of our meals free in exchange for my giving her daughter piano lessons and Leretta's helping with the kitchen. That was the way a lot of things were arranged in the thirties. People exchanged goods or services because cash was so short.

The success of the West Frankfort Grade School Band

also opened up another source of income for me. Other communities in the area soon heard about our band and wanted bands of their own. I made an arrangement with the Ludwig Music Company similar to the one I had had with Conn, and I began to go from town to town organizing bands. I would contact the superintendent or the school board members in a town and tell them I would establish a grade school band if they would let me have some space in one of their schools to teach the children when I came to town. I would always point out that the school would be getting a band and it wouldn't cost them anything, since the parents would be paying me directly. This usually sold them, and that's the way a lot of the bands in southern Illinois got started.

The first band that I established after West Frankfort was in Mt. Vernon. Since I had sold my Chevy, I would take the bus up there two days a week. I think the parents there paid me two dollars a month for a half-hour lesson a week for a child. Of course, I also got a small commission from the Ludwig Company for every instrument they were able to sell.

After Mt. Vernon I started a band in the little town of Golconda, Illinois. That was an experience for a boy from St. Louis used to the discipline and respect for authority of turn-of-the-century city schools. Golconda is on the Ohio River, and in those days it was full of tough rivermen and their equally tough children. It wasn't too unusual for one of those hulking big boys to threaten to clean my plow for me when I told him to do something he didn't like. I soon discovered, though, that if I could show these boys I was as tough as they were, they'd respect me.

One time in particular a big fellow went for me, and I ended up getting a half nelson on him.

"You can't do that," cried one of my girl students. "His father's on the school board."

Father on the board or not, I wrestled that big lad to a draw, and after that I had no more trouble with him. Later on his father came to see me.

"What did you do to my son?" he asked. "You can handle him better than I can."

I usually had excellent cooperation from the teachers and school administration when I went to a town, because they knew they were getting a good thing. But when I started a band in Du Quoin, Illinois, a town about thirty miles northwest of West Frankfort, the situation was different. For some reason the superintendent in Du Quoin didn't want a band in his school system. The school board and the parents supported me, so he had to let me use a school for lessons, but that didn't keep him from playing some cute tricks.

The bus I took to Du Quoin arrived at about four-thirty in time to work with the children after school, and I'd teach until I caught another bus back to West Frankfort at nine-thirty. In the winter it was almost dark by the time I got into town, so naturally we'd have to have the lights on at the school. This superintendent would come around and turn the lights out on us. He had to let us use the school, but by golly, he didn't have to let us use the lights!

For a while I overcame this little handicap by waiting until after the superintendent had left and then turning the lights back on. A friendly janitor would tip us off when the coast was clear. After a time, though, the superintendent got on to what I was doing, and he went me one better. When he got ready to leave he'd go around and take all the fuses out of the fuse boxes and put them in his pockets. Well, we had to have lights, so I worked out a system whereby all the children would bring coal-oil lamps from home when they came to their lessons. I think the superintendent eventually lost his job because of his hostility to music.

My main interest, however, continued to be the music program in West Frankfort. I kept the private lessons and band going all through 1931, and then at the start of the 1931–32 school year the school board hired me part time to bring the program officially into the school system. I got fifty-five dollars a month to teach two and a half days a week. The next year they were going to raise me to seventy-five a month, but I held out for a hundred and got it. Then in 1933–34 all the teachers had to take a 10 percent pay cut. Finally, in 1934–35 Miss Sorg resigned her job at the high school to go to Bloomington, Illinois, where her family lived, and I became a full-time music teacher by taking over the high school band as well. When that happened, I gave up my bands at the other schools.

Theodore Paschedag.

My flute teacher and good friend John Sauter.

H. A. Vandercook, founder and president of Vandercook College of Music.

The West Frankfort Grade School Band in 1930–31. This was the band that I formed for the C. G. Conn Company to present a concert in one month after I came to town. If you look closely, you will find the many saxophones buried in the last two rows. Notice also how the few wooden clarinets stand out among the metal ones.

The West Frankfort Grade School Band in 1935. By this time we
had acquired uniforms, sousaphones, and even a bassoon.

The West Frankfort High School Orchestra, 1937–38.

The West Frankfort High School String Octet played for many
civic and community functions during the late thirties.

The West Frankfort High School Band in 1940. This band was selected to compete in the National High School Band Contest in Battle Creek, Michigan.

Directing the West Frankfort Municipal Band in the fine new band shell in West Frankfort in 1951.

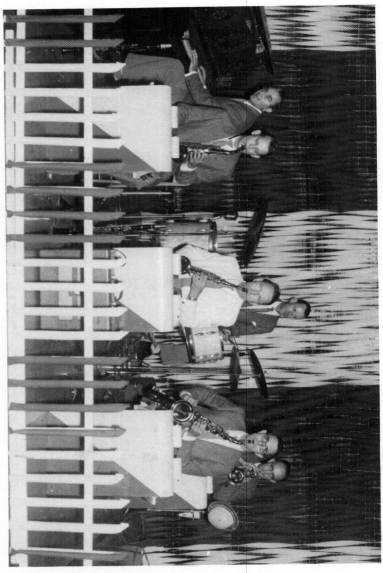

The dance orchestra that I played in, in 1958.

Directing the State Band of Oaxaca, Mexico, in one of its concerts played in the Oaxaca city square in 1966.

The State Band of Oaxaca, Mexico, July 1968.

A typical program of the State Band of Oaxaca.

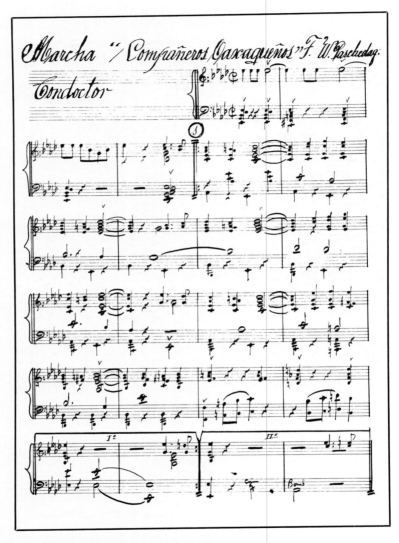

The conductor's score of "Compañeros Oaxaqueños," one of the marches I wrote for the State Band of Oaxaca.

Diego Innes, director of the State Band of Oaxaca, and I look over a score during a visit he made to West Frankfort in the late forties.

Directing the Southern Illinois Concert Band at the West Frankfort Fourth of July celebration, 1987.

There were a lot of problems in getting those early programs established and keeping them going. Before we were officially affiliated with the school system my West Frankfort band got no funds from it at all. Even when I was employed by the system there was precious little money available for the band. Yet a band is much more than just a group of people coming together with musical instruments; it needs money for music, for uniforms, and for a number of other purposes.

The most pressing need was for music. As the quality of the band improved we began to require more advanced material to play than that contained in *The Bennett Band Book*. I solved this problem by asking each child to bring fifty cents to band rehearsal, and we would pool this money to buy music. In those days fifty cents was a lot of money to some people, but somehow most of the children would show up with a fifty-cent piece or a couple of quarters. If they didn't, nothing was said, but that's the way I built up my band library.

A more difficult matter was intruments. Since each child owned his own instrument, he would naturally take it with him when he graduated, moved away, or dropped out. This didn't matter in the case of the smaller instruments like clarinets and cornets, because they were relatively cheap and there were always more children starting out on them to take the places of those who left. A large instrument like a bass horn or a baritone saxophone, however, was a different matter. It was a rare parent who could afford the price of one of these, and yet we needed them in the band, too. In almost all school bands today these instruments are owned by the school.

To get money for these larger instruments I turned to the town of West Frankfort. Right from the start I formed an active Band Boosters organization, and we chose as our motto my grandmother's saying, The Music Comes First. By that we meant that our first efforts would be directed toward goals that would help the children play better, i.e., getting the music and the instruments. When we had done all we could to those ends, then we would worry about what we considered nonessentials like uniforms, trips, etc.

With the help of the Band Boosters we did many of the things school bands even today do to raise money. We had car washes and bake sales and gave benefit concerts. The manager of the local movie theater, Mr. Barnett, had played piano in a theater orchestra, and he helped us a lot. Every Friday and Saturday we'd take a small group from the band down to the theater and give a performance outside. All the children were given theater tickets to sell, and we were supposed to get a small percentage of the price of each one for the band fund. Often, however, when we came to collect our money Mr. Barnett would give us all of the night's profits because he liked the band so much.

With help like that from a lot of people we were soon able to buy several melophones—substitutes for French horns in those days—a baritone horn, a tuba, and a bass drum, and we were in pretty good shape. Then we turned to the uniform problem. We got the parents to buy white trousers for the boys and white skirts for the girls. A local clothing store donated gold letter sweaters to the band, and another clothier gave us military-style forage caps in West Frankfort's other school color, purple, and there we had our uniforms. Maybe they weren't very fancy, but the band looked pretty sharp when it filled the stage for a concert.

When we became affiliated officially with the school system in the fall of 1931 a new problem arose. The people of West Frankfort had begun to take real pride in "their" band, and it wasn't long before I started to get pressure to enter it in the grade school band contest held every spring. At first I was against this. In those days there were no classes in grade school band competition. Our band that had been in existence less than two years would have to compete against well-established organizations from much larger schools. Our band was on the small side, too, as that year our number had shrunk to fifty- two. But what are you going to do? The people wanted the band in the contest, so finally I had to go along with it. I figured we'd do the best we could, and even if we could manage to get a second or a third place, it would be something for a band as new as ours.

In those days all the bands had to play one required number for the contest. That year it was a piece called, "Japanese Sunset." Then you could select a lighter number, and the third piece had to be a march. I had three very good flute players, so I chose a little gavotte called, "At the Spinet," which featured

48

some nice flute runs. For the march I selected Hall's "Officer of the Day," and that was our program when we went down to Carbondale, Illinois, for the contest.

Well, we did a pretty good job on those numbers, and we came back with a first place in that contest. The town went wild. There was a big story in the newspaper:

> "We went over to Carbondale buoyed up with the hope that we would bring home the bacon, but instead we brought home the whole hog," was the jubilant assertion of Theodore W. Paschedag, director of the grade school band while recounting the achievement of the band in the Southern Illinois District School Band Contest in Carbondale Saturday.
>
> The West Frankfort band, the smallest in number, the youngest in standpoint of activity, and a band nattily attired in the least conspicuous of uniform of any entry in the contest, came out winner of first honors. Harrisburg and Herrin shared honors with West Frankfort, but the local organization got the highest honor accorded all points considered.

I was also gratified by a letter I received from Mr. Henry Smith, the secretary-treasurer of Ludwig Music House in St. Louis, with whom I was working in establishing the other bands in the area. Mr. Smith wrote,

> I know you were thrilled with the performance of your band at Carbondale and proud of the splendid showing they made, and man you have every reason to be, for I never before witnessed such a big difference in any one band as I did in yours. Why the band that I heard in Carbondale performed like a professional band in every respect—Discipline, intonation, phrasing, and musicianship were perfect.

Praise like that from a man who made his living working with all kinds of school bands was not to be taken lightly.

The town gave us a big victory parade, and then it was back to work to get ready for the state contest at Springfield for which our Carbondale success had qualified us. Here we were up against twelve of the best bands in Illinois, almost all from larger towns such as Springfield, Champaign-Urbana, and several of the Chicago suburbs. We took top honors in what was called the third division there. I considered this very good, as all the other bands were much larger and had been in existence much longer than ours.

Our success in those two contests really solidified the grade school music program in West Frankfort. My telephone rang for days after we returned from the state contest. Every caller was a parent wanting to sign his son or daughter up for music lessons. From fifty-two the enrollment in band jumped to over two hundred the next year. Suddenly playing in the band was the "in" thing for the children of West Frankfort to do. In the next few years they would all get their chance, and there would be many other triumphs for our bands. None of these, however, would be more important than the honors we won that first year when we were just starting out in the contests.

S·I·X

THE NEXT FEW years in West Frankfort were some of the busiest and most rewarding in my life. The Great Depression was still going strong, so usually it was a struggle just to put groceries on the table, but I think there was a community spirit back then that we've somehow lost. Since nobody had any money, we all had to pitch in and find our own ways of getting joy out of life. I like to think that the music my bands played contributed its share to what happiness those overworked miners and farmers got from an existence that offered them so little in the way of material goods.

There was more of a community spirit among the music teachers in southern Illinois, too. We were constantly getting together to discuss our problems and sometimes just to play our instruments for the fun of it. Often we would take some of our students along to visit some other band's rehearsal and sit in. In those days a lot of band rehearsals were held at night, so we could do this. We'd also come to each other's concerts, and whenever you were in the audience, you could be sure the director would ask you to come up and guest-conduct a march. We were a real fraternity in those days.

I was also fortunate to have many opportunities to get in some playing myself. Shortly after I came to West Frankfort, what was then Southern Illinois Normal College and is now

Southern Illinois University–Carbondale started up an orchestra. There was no one at the college who played flute, so Mr. David McIntosh, the director, asked me to play with the group. A little later we formed an area string quintet. A Mrs. Philips of Benton had been a professional violinist and at one time was actually a violin soloist with the Sousa Band. Then a Mr. Swain, a retired theater violinist from St. Louis, moved to West Frankfort. His wife played piano. The sister of the Murphysboro, Illinois, band director—I think his name was McDaniels—was a good cellist, and we lured her to West Frankfort to teach strings in the grade school. So we had two violins, cello, flute, and piano, and we gave little musicales for teachers' meetings and civic groups and that kind of thing. And, of course, I was still playing for money in the dance orchestra out of Mt. Vernon.

Both Leretta and I lived and breathed music in those days. The house was continuously filled with young people who dropped in at all hours to practice or take lessons or just to talk. Leretta liked comic books and always had a lot of them lying around. Some youngsters would come an hour or two early for their lessons just so they could sit in our front room and read the comic books.

Leretta was wonderful with children. It never bothered her to have the house in a constant uproar and to have strange children constantly under foot. I'm sure I couldn't have gotten through those early years without her support. Although she was a good violinist, she gave up active playing when our two children were born, but she was part of every activity I took on, and every once in a while she would come down and rehearse a band when I had something else on.

One of her most concrete contributions was fitting drumheads. In the thirties you couldn't buy ready-fitted drumheads. All you got for your money were the treated skins. You had to cut and trim these and then fit them to the drums after they had been soaked in water so they would stretch tight when they dried. Leretta took on this job, and our basement was usually filled with pans of water with drumheads soaking in them. She got so good at fitting the heads that she began to do it for all the band directors in the area. In fact, the Ludwig

52

store in St. Louis once offered her a job as a drumhead fitter, but she turned it down.

There were many good times in those days, but I don't want to give you the wrong idea. It wasn't all flute quintets at faculty teas. Times were very hard, and there was a dark side to living in southern Illinois in the Great Depression. This area has a tradition of violence dating back at least as far as the labor conflicts that earned "Bloody Williamson" County just south of West Frankfort its name before the turn of the century. In the thirties the labor unrest returned, and to this was added gangsterism. Unlucky Williamson County was the territory of the notorious Berger Gang. This group added to its other illegal activities the only recorded incident of aerial bombardment within the continental United States when some of the boys dumped explosives out of a plane onto a roadhouse used as a headquarters by a rival gang.

Of course, as a band director I didn't have much part in most of this excitement, but it was impossible for anyone to escape it completely. When I finally got a car after a couple of years and began to drive to the towns where I gave music lessons, Mrs. Barrett, our landlady, would often tell me not to take certain roads on certain nights to avoid trouble. There were even some nights when you just didn't go out at all.

The labor troubles during that period centered naturally enough around the coal mines. Southern Illinois has always been very union oriented, and the majority of the people take union activities pretty seriously. In the early thirties the Progressive Mine Workers of America tried to take power away from the United Mine Workers Union, and this led to some pretty tense times. There were periodic outbreaks of violence, and the worst came in the fall of 1932. It even affected me.

Late one afternoon I started to walk from the school down to the postal express company, which was just off Main Street. Right next to the express office was Stone's Funeral Parlor, which was a United Mine Workers stronghold. As I approached this building, a man came out of its door and started down the steps. All at once another man stepped out from behind a tree and fired a pistol at the first fellow. The victim grabbed his chest and tumbled down the steps while the other man ran off. A group of people came running out of the funeral parlor and looked to the man who had been shot.

Maybe by rights I should have gone to help, too, but in those days it was far wiser not to get involved in that kind of thing if you could avoid it. I went on to the express office and did my business, and when I got back to school I went directly to Principal Waller and told him everything.

"You have family in St. Louis," he told me. "You're going to take a vacation. Get your wife and your children and leave right now. Somebody might have seen you watching that shooting and know you're a witness. They could be gunning for you. I'll fix it with the school board, and we'll let you know when to come back."

So Leretta and the children and I went to St. Louis where we stayed for two weeks before the principal sent word for us to return. In the meantime there had been a confrontation between the two unions. The Progressives, who were mainly from upstate, had organized an auto caravan to come down and "take over" southern Illinois. Leretta and I found out what happened to that effort on our way back from St. Louis. When we got to the little hamlet of Mulkeytown just outside West Frankfort we began to pass a long row of cars abandoned along the side of the road. Every one of them had had its tires shot out.

That abortive takeover was the high point of the Progressive movement in this part of the country, but feelings continued to run strong for some time. A little later the United Mine Workers held a big rally and invited their famous president, John L. Lewis, to speak. The Mine Workers wanted a band to play for the occasion, and since my grade school band played for everything, they asked us. I told the organizers we would play if they could guarantee the children's safety. They said not to worry.

I well remember that rally. The band marched down the street to the bandstand through a long corridor of men armed with rifles. There were also riflemen on the roofs of all the buildings around the area who kept watch through the entire concert. There was no trouble that day, and Mr. Lewis was thrilled with our band. He came down after his speech and talked with the children calling them, "my babies," since they were the sons and daughters of his miners. I think for Lewis our band was, in a way, tangible evidence of the good life he was trying to bring to the members of his union.

Throughout all this time my bands continued to play for just about every possible occasion. I instituted a summer music program, and the grade school band began to give weekly concerts at the bandstand on Main Street, which was located where the post office is now. This stand had been erected for the earlier community bands of the town and even had windows that could be put in place around it so the band could rehearse in bad weather. Every Thursday night the police would block off Main Street so that people could come and sit or stand or sit in their cars and hear the music. Later when the post office was built, the builders' unions donated their time to move the stand several blocks farther west along the street where we continued our concerts.

All this playing and the contests we continued to win began to pay off both in community interest and in publicity beyond the town and even southern Illinois. Tangible evidence of this came in the spring of 1934 when the grade school band was asked to represent the town and the area at the Chicago World's Fair during an "Egyptian Day." Southern Illinois is often known as "Egypt" or "Little Egypt," probably because of its proximity to Cairo, Illinois.

This seemed like a great opportunity to show off the band and probably the trip of a lifetime for many of those children of depression-squeezed miners and farmers. There was one big problem, however. It was going to take a lot of money to transport eighty-two children and enough parents to chaperon them to Chicago, put them up in a hotel, and bring them back. We estimated four hundred dollars, which was an immense sum in those days. I had my doubts we could raise it, but I called a meeting of the Band Boosters, and their verdict was, "Go for it."

We immediately set out to scrounge up the money, and the community support was just marvelous. The Band Boosters held ice-cream and lemonade sales and canvassed the town for donations. Two local baseball teams staged a "World's Fair" game with all the proceeds going to the band fund. Even John L. Lewis sent us fifty dollars out of his own pocket for his "babies." The fund grew slowly, but by July we knew we were going to make it. We were even able to arrange a special train on the Illinois Central Railroad to take us to Chicago. It is interesting to note that the final price for a round-trip ticket on this train from West Frankfort to Chicago —a distance of some six hundred miles—was $4.00 for adults and $3.50 for children. This was in August 1934.

At last all the arrangements were complete, and on August 10 the West Frankfort Grade School Band set out for Chicago. I had all the parents and children assemble at the Central School at 9:30 that night where I gave them some final instructions and passed out the tickets. Then we all went down to a private railroad siding belonging to the local Illinois Central Agent, where the train was waiting. The scene there was vividly described in a story that appeared the next day in the *Daily American:*

> While the train crew was going through the usual setting up exercises with the engine and baggage coach the parents lined up on either side of the three coaches that held their fondest hopes and, taking positions under the windows nearest their own flesh and blood, attempted with solemn face and warning voice, to impress upon their little darlings the dangers of sticking their heads out of the windows, running up and down the aisles and "acting smart." The kids stopped their giggling long enough to encourage their dads and moms with a quick nod of the head and an occasional, somewhat irritated, "al-right, al-right." . . . It was difficult to tell who among the holiday excursion crowd was having the most fun, the band members for whom the special was chartered or the parents who went along for ballast. The parental warning for the kids to stay out of the aisles was, it appeared, an unnecessary attempt to cope with imaginary danger. There was no room in the aisles for the kids. They were crowded with grinning papas and fair going mamas.

From the perspective of half a century the excitement generated by that excursion may seem a little quaint. Nowadays a trip to a large city, even by an eighty-four-piece grade

56

school band, is not an extraordinary occurrence. But in 1934, travel was not the easy matter it is today, even if the railroads were generally much better. Most of the children in my band — indeed, probably even some of the parents — had never been on a train before. Chicago for them was a dreamland somewhere beyond their ordinary experience of the world. In addition, we knew we were representing not just our own town but our whole area of the state to the "big city." Southern Illinoisans have always been keenly aware of being the "other Illinois," often patronized, denigrated, and sometimes just plain ignored by their more sophisticated neighbors in the metropolitan north. So not only did we want to have fun, we had something to prove.

We played three concerts in Chicago, and the children did me proud in all of them. The first was an Egyptian Day celebration at the Court of the States Theater the afternoon we arrived. Here we shared the program with the Du Quoin Drum and Bugle Corps, the Marion, Illinois, Grade School Band, and an All Southern Illinois Beauty Queen. The next afternoon we appeared at the Travel and Transport Building at the fair, and finally the last night of our stay we played in the lounge of the Allerton Hotel where we stayed. Between concerts the children were free to visit the fair.

The whole trip went off with very few problems. Probably the most exciting occurrence for me was when my son, Teddy, aged five, disappeared while we were visiting the fair. Fortunately, he turned up in a couple of hours holding on to the hands of some Boy Scouts and happily eating an ice-cream cone in the best tradition of lost little boys. Later the *West Frankfort Daily American* reported that Teddy had been lost, "probably while 'pop' was 'in the villages,' " the sideshow area of the fair that featured the famous fan dancer, Sally Rand, and I took a lot of kidding. For the record, I was nowhere near the "villages" when Teddy disappeared.

All in all the trip was a great success, although it was a pretty exhausted group of youngsters who had to be routed off the train when it got back to West Frankfort. It had taken a major community effort to raise the five hundred dollars necessary, but I think the people of West Frankfort got their money's worth. The band had given them something in which to take pride, and even those who stayed behind could share in a small way the pleasure of their children and the excitement of a world's fair and a big city. That may not seem like much in these days of easy television thrills, but in 1934 most people didn't ask for a great deal, and they got even less.

S·E·V·E·N

WHEN I JOINED the West Frankfort school system in 1931, I for the first time became conscious of my lack of formal education after high school. Not that I was by any means unique. Many of the school music teachers then were professionals who were without college educations. It was, perhaps, because of this that the state of Illinois allowed music teachers to get provisional teaching certificates simply by taking an examination. I took that exam early in the school year. It lasted for two days and was pretty thorough. I remember that among other tasks I had to write out all the fingerings for all the notes for all the instruments in the band. I was well prepared and passed it without much trouble, though.

But I still wasn't really satisfied with my status. There is a great deal of snobbery in public education, and I was constantly running into people who thought I couldn't possibly know my job, since I didn't have even a bachelor's degree. I decided that if I was going to make my career in education, I would have to play the game and get some letters to put after my name.

In the summer of 1932 an organization in Chicago, the Educational Music Bureau, sponsored a two-week music clinic in the city. A person could earn two academic credits through De Paul University for participating in it, so I thought it would be an easy way to get my feet wet in higher education. I played in both the band and the orchestra at this clinic, and both of these groups were led by men who were on the faculty of the Vandercook College of Music. I got to talking with them during breaks and over coffee, and both of them encouraged me to try for a degree at Vandercook during the summers.

H. A. Vandercook, the founder of Vandercook College had started his career as a virtuoso cornet player and the leader of circus bands. As he played and studied, he came to the conclusion that musical expression was an art that could be taught just as the fundamentals of playing an instrument can be taught. He published several instruction books on various aspects of playing and performing music, and in 1909 he bought the home of his late teacher, A. F. Weldon, in Chicago to open a school for professional musicians and band directors. He attracted first-rate men to his faculty, and the Vandercook College of Music quickly became known as the place to go for a sound, practical, musical education.

By the time I started attending Vandercook's five-week summer sessions the college had moved out of the old Weldon house to another big brownstone on Washington and Paulina streets. The teaching there reflected Hale Vandercook's philosophy of education. Every phase of music was taught very meticulously, and very little was left to the student's originality. Vandercook was a great believer in rules. At the college there was a rule for everything, including such matters as musical expression and interpretation. I remember taking band arranging from the old man, and every note on the staff and every line in my notebook had to be drawn just so.

Although Vandercook appeared gruff and forbidding at first, I quickly got to know him, and we developed a warm friendship that lasted until his death in 1949. He had a sense of humor, too, and a way of getting his point across. He used to give his private lessons on the third floor of that old brownstone house, and there is a story about one of his cornet students who insisted upon rushing a slow passage Vandercook had given him for a lesson. Finally, exasperated, H. A. stopped the fellow and said, "Blow the first note of this piece — just the first note."

60

The boy blew the note.

"Now go downstairs to the steps outside this building and blow the second note," H. A. ordered. "Then come back here."

The boy tramped down all three flights of stairs, went out the front door, blew the note, and then climbed back up the three flights of stairs to the lesson room again.

"Fine," said Vandercook when the student once again stood before him puffing and wheezing. "Now blow the third note."

The boy blew the third note, and Vandercook then ordered him to go back downstairs and out on the steps and blow the fourth. Up and down the stairs the poor student went, blowing note after note until he had played about four bars of his assignment. Finally, when he once again stood before his teacher, gasping and exhausted, the old man fixed him with his eagle eye and said, "Now that is what I mean when I say play that passage *slowly!*

At the time I attended the college the faculty was just first-rate. Vandercook's protégé and aid, H. E. Nutt, taught there. Forest, "Frosty" Buchtel instructed in trombone, and Clifford Lillya taught cornet. John Beckerman, a very fine clarinet and flute player, headed the woodwind faculty, and Joe Olivadoti taught arranging, composition, and also oboe. Ralph Lewis had the strings, and advanced clarinet students could study under Lillia Paenish who at that time was first clarinetist with the Chicago Symphony Orchestra. All of these people in the course of time became good friends of mine, and I owe a great deal of my knowledge of music to their instruction.

H. A. Vandercook himself led the college band, which met every morning at eleven o'clock. His repertoire consisted mainly of the great band music of the past that he had played and loved as a band director. As in everything, he was a meticulous conductor, precise and easy to follow. In the book he had written on conducting he told his students that the day of the romantic, individualistic conductor more intent on showing off than in obtaining a good performance was over, and he followed his own advice.

Attending Vandercook College was a great experience for me. The school was so small—there were only about fifty or so students while I was there—that it was really more like being

61

part of a fraternity than a student body. All the students either were, or were going to be, school band directors, so we were serious about our studies, and we had that magnificent faculty to work with us. In addition, we were encouraged to attend as many musical events in Chicago as we could after classes. Old H. A. Vandercook would sometimes even order us to go to concerts directed by people he considered bad conductors.

"Tonight you'll see the worst conductor in Chicago," he'd tell us. "Go watch him and learn how not to do it."

Besides the five-week summer sessions, I took some correspondence courses in music theory and arranging from Vandercook and from Indiana University. I filled in the academic side of my college education by taking some extension courses offered by Southern Illinois Normal University at Carbondale. Then I attended two summer sessions in Carbondale where I minored in geology, a subject that has always interested me. Finally, on July 29, 1937, I was awarded a B.A. degree in music from Vandercook. I kept taking courses in music, mostly through correspondence, working with Guy Holmes of Vandercook, and two years later I was granted a master of music degree.

My association with H. A. Vandercook didn't end when I finished my college work, however. Hale and I had become well acquainted from the work I had done in his bands and classes, and we discovered that we had many things in common besides music, which in itself would have been enough to bring us together. My wife also became great friends with his wife, Emily, whom he and everyone else called "Auntie Van." The Vandercooks had a cottage on Lake Catherine just north of Chicago, and we would frequently spend weekends there together fishing and talking. Leretta would drive Auntie Van up there early on Friday, and then I would bring H. A. When Friday classes at Vandercook were over. H. A. loved nature and fishing almost as much as he loved music, and since these are also two of my loves, we got along very well together.

Vandercook felt a real bond with nature. He loved to go out in the woods or sit along the bank of a lake. I remember one morning coming out of the cabin to find him sitting on the shore with his fishing rod and a little black snake beside him.

"Don't bother this little fellow," he told me. "He's a friend of mine."

Vandercook also had little time for people who didn't display the proper respect for the outdoors and especially for fishing. One time he and I were out on the lake fishing from his boat when a motorboat came roaring up, sending a huge wake and ruining the fishing for the moment. It was a game warden come to check our licenses.

"Keep your license in your pocket," Vandercook growled to me. "Let me do the talking to that damn fool who doesn't know enough to cut his engine when he comes up to people fishing."

"How do I know you're a game warden?" he growled after the fellow had asked to see our credentials. The man pointed to the very official looking star on his jacket.

"Any damned fool can make himself a star," H. A. snorted. "We used to cut them out of tin cans when I was a kid. I don't think you're a real game warden. You don't even know how to approach a fisherman properly. If you were a real warden, you'd show some respect for the lake and the fish."

And he spent half an hour lecturing the fellow on proper boat courtesy. The warden finally went off considerably humbled, and we never did have to show him our licenses, although I had my hand on my billfold a number of times.

One of Vandercook's more interesting possessions was a large, green parrot named Yucatan. Old H. A. was as fond of a nip now and then as he was of music, and he had a favorite tavern not far from the college to which he often repaired for a bit of "tonic" as he called it. One day he was enjoying one when he spotted this big parrot that belonged to the bartender. H. A. decided that he had to have that parrot. The bartender didn't mind selling the bird, but he warned Vandercook that some of his patrons had taught it some pretty salty language.

Yucatan turned out to be an excellent talker, and the only really off-color phrase he knew was "damned Democrat," a label he would apply to anyone who got him angry. He was a touchy bird and was not above giving one a nip of his beak now and then, although he loved to have the top of his head scratched. When Vandercook died, I more or less inherited

Yucatan. I kept him in my yard, and he'd sit there screeching at the people who passed by. He and Leretta got along famously, and he died one Christmas day while she held him in her lap. In a way, he was almost as much a character as his original master.

I also spent a lot of time driving Mr. Vandercook around. At one time H. A. had a driver's permit, and he was fond of telling people how to drive, but he would never get behind the wheel himself. The story goes that sometime before I met him he had bought himself a Model A Ford and had started to take lessons from Auntie Van. H. A. was doing pretty well until one day he met another car on the road. Vandercook panicked and drove off into a cornfield. No damage was done to either car or occupants, but H. A. was completely shaken.

"Auntie Van!" he roared, "Get behind the wheel and drive that S.O.B.!" And he never drove again.

In 1929 Vandercook and his college faculty had started a summer music camp at Bridgeman, Michigan, for both band directors and their students. This was one of the first of this type of camp. Vandercook had a complete program of study for students from junior high age to their teachers, and it was possible to earn credit at Vandercook College for attending the camp. The two-week affair was held at a Congregational Church campground that Vandercook rented. Often we would play our final concert in the Congregational Church of Bridgeman because of its good acoustics.

I attended this camp one year as Vandercook's assistant, and the next year he turned its direction over to me. From 1935 to 1942 I directed the camp, and I feel we had an excellent program in both band and orchestra. Vandercook then went on to set up camps at Colorado, Texas, Iowa, Mississippi, South Dakota, and other places in Michigan, and I went with him to almost all of them. Usually they were held in late July or early August, so I would be able to finish my own summer music program in West Frankfort before going on the road. It was a great way to spend a vacation, doing the work I loved and getting paid for it at the same time.

In 1941 Vandercook retired from Vandercook College and settled in his wife's old home at Allerton, Michigan. He still kept in touch with the school, however, through his protégé,

H. E. Nutt, and he made sure the teaching there was always in accordance with his theories of practical music education. Leretta and I drove up to see him as often as we could. He remained bright and alert until his death. He was one of the most remarkable men and musicians I have ever met. Music education in America owes a great deal to H. A. Vandercook.

E·I·G·H·T

WITH MISS SORG'S resignation in the fall of 1935, I was given full charge of the instrumental music program in the West Frankfort schools, which made me responsible for the four grade schools, the so-called Central School, and for both the high school band and the orchestra. Although this meant a lot of work, it also meant that I could shape the program pretty much to suit myself. I worked out a system that I felt would give me the very best possible musicians by the time the children reached high school.

Although most of my students started music lessons in about the fourth grade, I made it a rule that I would accept a child whenever he or she wanted to start. I felt that if a child had an interest in music and a desire to play, there was no reason to make him wait until some arbitrary age. I also made it a practice to allow my students to play the instrument they themselves selected. I know that many music teachers feel that the instructor should try to match each student with the instrument that is best suited to his physical makeup, but I always felt that if a student had the desire, he would overcome any physical handicaps and no matter how well an instrument suited him, if he didn't want to play it, he wouldn't do well on it.

I spent my mornings during the school year at the grade schools and the Central School giving sectional rehearsals, and my afternoons at the high school. The high school band rehearsed the last period of the afternoon. It was the only organization that rehearsed as a group during the school day. The grade school band and the high school orchestra rehearsed on Tuesday nights. Since almost all of my students were also taking private lessons from me during the other evenings of the week, the music program obviously demanded a good deal of commitment from my students. I always tried to gear my teaching as though every child would someday become a professional musician. Some people criticized me for this, but I always felt that you never knew what would become of any given student.

This kind of program was also, of course, very demanding on me personally. I was willing to do it, because I felt that to be a good teacher you have to be dedicated to your subject and your students. Teaching is not a profession in which you can just go and punch a time clock and then leave and forget it at the end of the day. I think part of our problem in music education today is that not enough teachers are willing to give it the devotion it demands.

And speaking of devotion, we certainly couldn't have had a successful program in West Frankfort if it hadn't been for the complete cooperation of the school officials, the other teachers, and especially the parents and townspeople. If the parents hadn't made sure their children practiced, if they hadn't been willing to give them up for two night rehearsals a week, and if they hadn't been enthusiastic about music, my program would never have had a chance. I think more parents today should realize that the most dedicated teachers can't do much unless they have the parents behind them. A community gets the kind of educational system it's willing to pay for, and that means not only in terms of money but also in terms of emotional support. If a community wants its school system to be an athletics machine, it will get that kind of program. If it wants its schools to teach art and culture, sooner or later the schools will succeed in teaching these subjects.

In the thirties West Frankfort was willing to make the commitment to music. As I said before, when I took over the grade school music program I had the grade school band playing for all kinds of community activities to make the town feel that it was their band, and when I went into the high school I continued this practice with the high school band. My superintendent, C. A. Waller, was a great help in this. In those days bands didn't play for football games and did little marching. There was, however, a marching section in the state contest, so the high school band did have to practice street drill a little. Superintendent Waller loved to have us march, and often on a nice spring or fall day he would tell me in the morning to have the children bring their uniforms when they came back from lunch, and during band period we'd put on an impromptu parade on Main Street.

Most people in town enjoyed seeing the band march, and it was good advertising for us. Once in a while, though, the marching had unforeseen results. Once I was accosted at one of the local Lions Club luncheons by another member who had a shop on Main Street. This fellow had a gorgeous secretary working for him, and it was well known that for years he had been unsuccessfully trying to have an affair with her.

"Paschedag!" he roared as he came up to me. "I'm going to kill you! You know how long I've been trying to get my secretary to go to bed with me."

I confessed that I had heard the rumor.

"Well, last Tuesday I finally got her to go upstairs to the little bedroom over my shop. We both got all excited and were just about ready to get in the sack, when what do you think? All of a sudden there was the whole damn West Frankfort High School Band right underneath my window blaring out, "The Stars and Stripes Forever" march. That got us both so shook that after that I couldn't get anything romantic done at all. Five years of the hardest seducing I ever tried down the drain!"

Laughing, I apologized and promised him we'd try to play something a little softer the next time we marched past his store.

With all the support that I had, it was little wonder that the West Frankfort bands continued to do well in the music contests during those years. These contests were more strongly influenced by the music profession in those days than they are now. The judges, for example, were more likely to be musicians from a professional orchestra instead of other band directors. Also, the contests tended to be much closer to the concert experience than they are now. Because of the interest in instrumental music many more parents and spectators attended, and it was customary for the band directors to keep their students in the hall after they had performed to listen to other bands. Thus, when you did your contest numbers you were playing for a large audience rather than for three people hidden away somewhere in the back of a nearly empty hall.

In the thirties the district contests were usually held in Carbondale or one of the other larger towns. The state grade school contest was in Bloomington or Springfield. The state high school contest was almost always in Champaign and centered around the University of Illinois and its great band led by Professor A. A. Hardin. This contest took up two weekends, one for the soloists and one for the bands. One wonderful aspect of the high school contest was that on the Saturday of the solo contest the University of Illinois Band would present a two-hour concert for all the children. This was a great help to us band directors, because our students could hear a living example of the kind of musical experience we were trying to teach them to create.

For many of my students those state contests were one of the most important events of the school year. I had a first-baritone-horn player one year who insisted on playing with the band even though he had been running temperatures of 104 degrees for several days before. Another time disaster almost struck when my first six grade-school clarinet players all came down with the measles a day or two before the contest. In those days measles meant strict quarantine, but our local doctor, Dr. Eldridge, was a big supporter of the band. He told us to get the girls dressed in their uniforms, put heavy powder on their faces, and drive them to the contest in a private car. They stayed in the car until it was time for the band to play, went in and played, and then were hustled right back into the car again and were driven straight home. Nobody outside the band knew the girls were sick, they were none the worse for the trip, and best of all, the band got a first.

When I first came to West Frankfort, southern Illinois took little part in the professional music educators' organizations, the Music Educators' National Convention and the Illinois Music Educators' Association. I.M.E.A. was mainly an organization for vocal music teachers, and it was dominated by the northern part of the state. Then in March 1944, the M.E.N.C. held its national convention in St. Louis, and the members of the I.M.E.A. decided that this would be a good time to reorganize and include instrumental as well as vocal teachers. I was honored to be elected the first president of the new I.M.E.A., an office I held for three years until succeeded by Ray Dvorack, the director of the Eastern Illinois University Band. By that time we had firmly established the new organization as an association that represented all music teachers on a statewide basis, and it remains this way today.

The year after I took the presidency, the I.M.E.A. selected West Frankfort as the site for its annual band clinic, and several thousand music teachers and students came from all over the state for this three-day event. The highlight of the clinic was a concert by the then-famous Joliet, Illinois, Grade School Band. This band came to town in its own private Pullman railroad cars and stayed overnight in them.

It is interesting to note that in those days many of the members of the I.M.E.A. were school orchestra leaders. There were many more orchestras in the state back then, and I established one in West Frankfort shortly after I took over the high school program. The I.M.E.A. held regular orchestra contests in the thirties. I think the decline of the school orchestras has been a big loss to school music programs. This happened, I think, partly because it takes a lot longer to become proficient on a string instrument and students lost the patience to put in this necessary practice as more activities arose to challenge music. Also, many of the string teachers were more interested in teaching one or two talented "artists" among their students than in establishing general programs as the band men were willing to do.

In the thirties the M.E.N.C. also sponsored a national high school band contest that was very prestigious. A band had to win its local district contest, its state contest, and then be recommended to get to go to the national contest. In 1940 the West Frankfort Band was fortunate enough to get this recommendation. By that time many of the children I had started in grade school had reached high school, and we had an excellent band. We were especially strong in woodwinds, and our big contest number was the *William Tell* Overture, which is far from an easy piece for high school students. I remember we got a standing ovation and four curtain calls when we finished it at the district contest in Champaign.

That year the national contest was held in Battle Creek, Michigan. The West Frankfort School Board scraped together a little money, and the band raised some so we could take some private cars along with a bus. Our principal, Sam Sullivan, and I took turns driving the bus, because we couldn't afford to pay a regular driver. We left West Frankfort at three o'clock in the morning and reached Battle Creek at six that afternoon. Then occurred one of the most bizarre and funny incidents in my entire career as a music teacher.

The committee that ran the national contest had arranged to put the members of the competing bands in private houses during their stay in Battle Creek. When we got to the city, Mr. Sullivan and I began dropping our children off at the houses assigned to them. Sullivan had been there before, so he thought he had a pretty good idea of where all the addresses we had been given were located. We set off with a carload of little girls, but without knowing it the principal got his directions mixed and instead of going to the north side of town as we should have we ended up on the south side. We pulled up before an elegant old house that looked like a private residence but was actually a house of ill fame. Honest to goodness, it was a bawdy house!

In perfect innocence Sullivan and I walked up and knocked at the door, which was opened by a slightly overdressed but kindly looking lady who was the madam.

"Hello," said Principal Sullivan cheerfully, "I imagine you've been expecting us."

The "lady" gave him a slightly puzzled look, but her establishment was ready for anything. "No," she said, "we weren't, but come on in anyway. How many of you are there?"

By the time the school girls got out of the car and came up to the door the horrible truth was beginning to dawn. The madam was very nice about the whole thing. She talked to the girls a little about their music and gave us directions to our real destination, which we quickly found without further trouble. Poor Sam Sullivan, though, was a marked man from then on. For years afterward people would kid him about trying to deliver a carload of his innocent students to a bawdy house.

Once we got the sleeping accommodations sorted out, the contest was a big thrill for us. The evening before the judging, the competing bands marched around the huge Kellogg Stadium to a drum cadence. Each band would then stop and play a march. We were not judged on the marching, but there were judges present who evaluated us and gave us suggestions for improvement. Our band played Sousa's "Manhattan Beach," and one of the judges said it sounded just the way it did when Mr. Sousa played it, a real compliment.

The next day the judging started in earnest. One of the first events for us was the sight-reading competition. Then another strange thing happened. We had hardly started playing when our tympani player, George Castleton, developed a nosebleed. We tried everything to stop it but with no luck. Luckily there were some people in the building who knew about pressure points and that sort of thing, and finally they got the flow of blood stopped and packed George's nose. We only had three drummers with the band, and without George we couldn't play. The contest officials, however, allowed us to wait for George and scheduled another band to play in our place. When George had rested for a bit, we went ahead and did our sight-reading, and it actually worked out pretty well, because our band had some extra time to warm up. I had a letter from George Castleton just last year in which he asked if I remembered his bloody nose at the national contest. He said he wasn't nearly so worried about the nosebleed as about the possibility he wouldn't be able to play.

After the sight-reading we did our prepared numbers in a large concert hall. We must have played pretty well, because when the contest was over we came out in third place among the thirty or so bands competing. Third place in the nation was not bad for a little town in southern Illinois and the smallest band in the contest. It firmly established West Frankfort's reputation as a music center in Illinois and was a tremendous boost to our program. And it didn't hurt to have Principal

Sullivan along, either. He was impressed by the resources of some of the other bands from larger schools. When we got home he pressured the school board for a hefty increase in my band budget.

The coming of the Second World War brought many changes to our music programs in Southern Illinois and some in my own private life. Many of the students that I had taught in high school were quickly scattered all over the globe playing in service bands. One of the first casualties of the war were the annual music contests. These had to be discontinued, because with gas rationing and the restrictions on travel it was simply impossible for bands to assemble in central places like Carbondale and Champaign. To keep up interest in the West Frankfort schools I substituted intramural contests, giving silver cups to the best high school and grade school musicians each year.

The war also made it extremely difficult to obtain supplies and especially instruments. The instrument companies simply stopped making new instruments for the duration. All of a sudden used horns were at a premium, and we scoured attics and basements throughout southern Illinois to try to buy them for our students. In fact, the major instrument companies did the same thing, and there was some hard feeling here because these companies were buying up all the local instruments to sell to other parts of the country.

Even before Pearl Harbor the music companies seemed to neglect southern Illinois, and it was hard to get music and reeds and all of the other incidentals that are so necessary to keeping a band playing. I was able to help the other band directors a bit with this problem because of my early connections with the Conn and Ludwig companies, and some of them began to encourage me to open up a music store, since the area needed one so badly. It seemed like a good idea, so in 1941, just before the war came, the Paschedag Music Company was born.

At first Leretta and I operated the store right from our house. Then in 1943 the father of one of my saxophone players, a Mr. Rodenbush, offered to rent me a little store on Main Street just across the street from the high school for all of fifteen dollars a week. I jumped at the chance, because it was such a wonderful location. I was right there whenever any of my high school students needed to buy anything, and business was excellent. This was especially true just after the war when new instruments were starting to be manufactured again, but there was still a shortage. I can remember many times when the express man would come to my store and people would be lined up on the sidewalk outside waiting to see if the boxes he brought contained the instruments they had ordered.

We kept trying to increase the services we could offer to our customers, and just after the war I hired a young man named Lester Talbot from Mt. Vernon as a full-time instrument repairman. We started doing all kinds of repair jobs even to completely relacquering and reconditioning horns. Lester stayed with Leretta and me until he got married to a girl from Springfield and moved there. After that we tried a couple of other fellows for a while and then pretty much got out of the repair business. There was less and less call for complete reconditioning jobs anyway. With the increased cost of lacquer and other raw materials we were having to charge our customers so much that they might just as well buy a brand new instrument.

In addition to Lester I also hired a high-school girl, Freda Pirtle, to help out in the music store. Freda began working just after school, but I trained her and for many years she worked full time. She is back to part-time work now, but after thirty-three years she knows as much about the business as I do. I doubt if either of us realized when she first came into the store in 1952 that we would both be tending it so long afterward. We kept that little store on Main Street going for a number of years and then moved into a former furniture store farther down the street. The Paschedag Music Company is still doing business there today.

After the war ended the state and district contests started up again in southern Illinois. Our bands competed in them for a few years, but I began to get disenchanted with the contest as a teaching aid. If you go to a contest, you go to win, and as the competition increased it began to mean spending more and more time rehearsing the contest numbers every year. It got to the point that you almost had to spend the whole school year preparing just three pieces. Some of this kind of polishing

75

is good, but I always liked to have my bands play a lot of concerts and introduce my students to a variety of kinds and styles of music.

Then too, the judging of the contests was moving out of the hands of professional musicians into those of people in academia, especially those in college and university music departments. I am not saying that these people were inferior to the prewar professional judges, but they had different standards and they looked for different things in the bands they heard. I did not share their outlook, because I myself am from the profession. I began to feel more and more out of touch at contest time.

Finally, I stopped taking my bands to contest at all. I reinstituted the intramural contests I had held during the war, and to show off the high school band I took it on tours. I was able to get permission to take the children out of school on a Thursday and a Friday, the days they normally would have had off for contest, and we were able to arrange three-day tours that got back to West Frankfort on a Saturday night.

A couple of years we went south into Kentucky and Tennessee. Once we played an afternoon concert in Chattanooga, and afterward the principal of our host high school took the whole band, still in uniform, out to the Civil War cemetery there and explained to the children the history of the war in that area. He did this because I had told him that our band members all had to write papers on the history of Chattanooga when they got back to West Frankfort. Another time we went north and played concerts in Rantoul and Champaign, Illinois.

By this time we had developed a nearly complete musical program in West Frankfort. In addition to rehearsing the various bands and the high school orchestra, I was also teaching some classes in music theory and harmony, and each year we put on a complete musical show. I had started the musicals back in the thirties. For a time we had a very fine vocal music teacher, Neva Gloyd, who was also an excellent pianist. She and I got together, and the first show we did was Gilbert and Sullivan's *Mikado*. After that we did one show a year, complete with pit orchestra and the whole works. It was another kind of musical experience we could offer our students.

For many years, then, I was very happy in West Frankfort as the music teacher. But in 1951 I decided to bring it all to a halt. By then I had spent twenty-one years as a teacher in the school system. Since I was eligible for retirement, I decided to take it. The salary the school board was willing to offer me wasn't as much as I thought it should be, and I felt I could do better by living on my retirement and concentrating on the music store. Besides, I could see changes coming in music education. More and more, the public and the schools were beginning to emphasize athletics, and with this came a demand that the school music programs be geared to support the athletic programs. Bands were now expected to spend almost half the school year preparing half-time shows for football games. I have nothing against marching bands, but I have always felt that the major purpose of a school band is to play concerts of serious music. I wanted to be a music educator and not just an entertainer. I could see, however, that I was bucking a trend so I got out. I do think, though, that many of the problems we see in music education today got their start with the growing emphasis on athletics in the early fifties.

Thus in 1952 I stepped down as band director at West Frankfort. I had devoted twenty-two years of my life to the music program in this little city. I had raised my two children there and lost one of them. We had lost dear little Teddy in 1935 when he was struck by a car while out selling tickets to raise money for the grade school band in which he played drums. My daughter, Bea, had started out playing E-flat clarinet, because her hands were too small for the standard B-flat model. When she got a little older I switched her to the larger instrument, and then when we needed it she had taken up the bass clarinet. She was married now, and Leretta and I were on our own. Even though I was stepping down as bandmaster, she and I felt that we had become part of the town. Thus I was not about to fade off to some retirement village or old people's home. We still had the music store. West Frankfort wasn't through with us yet.

N·I·N·E

I HAVE ALWAYS HAD a keen interest in the Spanish language and Spanish culture. This probably stems from the year I spent with my Aunt Emily in St. Louis. My aunt's husband, Uncle Ed Nolan, was employed as a plumber on the locks of the Panama Canal. The conditions of his job called for him to spend every third year back in the United States, and this is why he and my aunt were in St. Louis when I came back from Labaddie to go to high school.

For a while my aunt and uncle planned to take me with them to Panama when they went back. They urged me to take all the Spanish I could in high school and to get some private lessons so that I would be able to speak the language some when I got there. By the end of my freshman year, though, I had developed my interests in music and printing, and my grandmother came back from California, so I could stay with her after Uncle and Aunt left.

I always tried to keep up with my Spanish, however, by listening to Spanish-language broadcasts on the radio and conversing with people who knew the language when I could. Fortunately, when I came to West Frankfort there were two excellent Spanish teachers in the school system, Mrs. Grace Wilson and Mrs. Alice Hoye, so I could speak Spanish with them and talk about the culture as much as I wanted.

Nothing much came of this until 1940 when Leretta's mother moved to California. That summer we started to drive out there to visit her. We got to a place in Missouri where the road forks, one branch going on west to California and the other turning south to Mexico by the newly opened Pan-American Highway. I stopped the car and said to Leretta, "Do you really want to go to California?"

"I don't know," she said. "You've been talking about Mexico for years. I'd kind of like to go there."

We talked a little, and finally I got out of the car and flipped a quarter into the air. Heads we would go to Mexico; tails and it was on to California. The quarter came up heads, so off we went south to Mexico. I suppose if that quarter had landed tails a whole interesting part of my life might never have come to be.

The Pan-American Highway was still pretty primitive, but Leretta and I really enjoyed that trip. We got as far as Mexico City where we went out to Chapultepec Park and heard the Mexico City Police Band, which was famous then. Because I was a band director we were able to go up after the concert and meet the leader and some of the musicians. They were very nice to us and told us to be sure to come back to Mexico City whenever we could.

After that we were hooked. The next summer we went back to Mexico and visited not only Mexico City but several other towns as well. We probably would have made it an annual journey but with the coming of the war such long trips were out of the question. In addition Mexico itself came under a cloud in this country. The Nazis had been very active there in the late thirties, and with my German-sounding name and the fact that I had made two trips there some people in West Frankfort had even come up with the idea that I might be a spy for Hitler.

My ties with Mexico were maintained in a rather unusual way during that time, however. One Sunday morning I happened to notice a story in the newspaper about a young man who had walked into Herrin Hospital the night before with a high fever and chills. This fellow could not speak English, and nobody at the hospital could understand him. They thought, though, that his name was Pedro and the language he was speaking was Spanish. The hospital asked the help of anyone who spoke that language.

I called up Mrs. Hoye, and we drove to the hospital and found that Pedro was a young Mexican who was up here working on the railroad. His last name was Acusto and he had had little education. We got things straightened out for him at the hospital, and I made a lifelong friend. After that every once in a while Pedro would drop in on Leretta and me. When he still couldn't speak English he would write my address on a piece of paper, flag down a bus, and give the paper to the driver who would let him off in West Frankfort. We'd have long talks in Spanish about his homeland, and sometimes when he could stay a little longer I'd take him down to school with me. He used to get quite upset with my students, because he thought they didn't give me enough respect.

Finally when his work visa ran out, Pedro had to go back to Mexico, but he continued to keep in touch with me. Later he returned to the United States and wandered around a lot. He eventually ended up in Gary, Indiana, working in the steel mills. He died there in 1947 from tuberculosis that he had had for a long time without knowing it. He was really a very intelligent boy and a good representative of his country while he was here. I never regretted that Sunday morning when I drove down to the Herrin hospital on a whim.

In addition to Pedro we had another young Mexican, Vincente de la Rose, as a visitor during those years. Vincente's brother was attached to the Mexican embassy in Washington, and our high school Spanish teachers met him on a trip there. When they found out that he had three brothers who wanted to visit the United States they invited them to West Frankfort, and I volunteered to take in Vincente. Actually, he was the only one of the three to come. Their parents had looked at a map of the U.S., and it appeared to them that West Frankfort was very near Chicago. In their part of Mexico, Chicago had the reputation of being full of gangsters so they were afraid to let the younger brothers go near it.

By the time the war ended, then, my interest in Mexico was even stronger. As soon as travel became possible again

Leretta and I headed south intending not only to visit Mexico but to go on south as far as Guatemala. But the American embassy in Mexico City discouraged this, and we settled for driving as far as the Mexican city of Oaxaca, about sixty miles south of Mexico City. At that time Oaxaca was a beautiful little town of about thirty-five thousand, and we fell in love with it immediately. It was very clean and almost untouched by tourists, and the prices were very low. I think five dollars got us three meals a day in the excellent hotel on the central square.

We got into Oaxaca on a Friday afternoon. In the hotel lobby I happened to meet a professor from the local university who agreed to act as a guide for us. He took us around and showed us all the sights, especially the grave of the hero Juárez whom the Mexicans call the father of their country. Then we went back to the hotel and got a good night's sleep.

The next morning I went out for a stroll around the square that the hotel fronted, and the first thing I saw was a man with a trumpet case under his arm sitting on one of the benches having his shoes shined. I went up to him and introduced myself as an American and a musician. He seemed delighted to see me and told me that he played first trumpet in La Banda de Musica del Estada Oaxaca (the State Band of Oaxaca), which would be giving a concert in the square on Sunday afternoon. He said for me to be sure to attend it so he could introduce me to its assistant director, Senior Mozis Baltazar, who would be conducting because the director, Diego Innes, was away in Mexico City.

We made it a point to be in the square when it was time for that concert. There, a good-sized band was getting ready to play, and sitting in the first-trumpet chair was my friend of the day before. As soon as he saw me he broke into a big smile and motioned for me to come up to the stand. I did so, and he introduced me to the conductor, Senior Baltazar. When I told Baltazar that I was a bandleader and played flute he had a chair brought forward and sat me down right there on the stand next to the first-clarinet player so I could watch his music. And there I sat, probably the only gringo in Oaxaca aside from Leretta, through that whole two-hour concert.

Bands were and still are very popular in Mexico, and that square was packed with peasants who had come in from the countryside just for the concert. They formed a very knowledgeable and appreciative audience.

When the concert was over I thanked Senior Baltazar for his kindness, and we talked a little more about music and bands. He said a few things I didn't quite catch, but that didn't bother me. My Spanish was far from perfect, and I didn't always understand what was being said to me. Finally, the two of us said, "Adios," the musicians departed, and Leretta and I went back to the hotel for supper. I thought that would be the end of my experience with the Stand Band of Oaxaca.

The next morning, however, as we were having breakfast at the hotel, here came a couple of Mexicans on bicycles.

"You are supposed to be Senior Baltazar's guest at the band rehearsal at the convent this morning," they told me. "We have been waiting for you."

That was what the conductor had been trying to tell me after the concert, and I hadn't understood!

One of the Mexicans offered me his bicycle to ride to the convent. When we arrived there, the band was in full stride and all of the schoolchildren in Oaxaca were there because they were practicing for a festival. I had hardly walked through the door when Senior Baltazar called me up to the podium.

"Here," he said, handing me the baton, "you conduct the rest of the rehearsal."

Well, you can imagine how I felt. I hadn't the slightest idea of what a Mexican band expected out of its conductor, and I wasn't even sure I could communicate with the musicians that well. Fortunately, when I looked through the program I found that it consisted mainly of numbers I had played many times before. The overture, I remember, was *Beautiful Galatea* with its lovely horn and oboe solos. Senior Baltazar was insistent, so at last I took the baton and he walked to a chair in the back of the room and sat down.

Once I got started, I began to feel right at home with that band. After all, music is music no matter what language the players speak. I decided early on that I wouldn't pull my punches. If I wasn't happy with the way the musicians played a passage, I stopped them and made them do it over. I guess I figured that if they didn't like it, what could they do, fire me?

I worked that band for over an hour, and when I was through I congratulated them on being fine musicians and real artists, which they were. The band members all seemed friendly and appreciative, and the first-oboe player, Senior Priscilliano Martinez Mota, came up and introduced himself to me. He invited me to come with him and Senior Baltazar to the local cafe for a *copita* (a little drink). Our little drink lasted some two hours as we sat and discussed music and our two cultures. When we finally parted, I knew I had made two firm friends.

During our talk Senior Baltazar insisted that I guest-conduct a number at the concert the next Sunday. Leretta and I had planned to leave Oaxaca before then, but how could we disappoint our new friends? We stayed, and I conducted *Orpheus in the Underworld* by Offenbach. It was a real thrill to conduct that group, not only because it was Mexican, but also because it was such an excellent band. The caliber of musicianship was very high, and the band played what was then pretty much the standard band repertory in the United States, works like *Ballet Egyptien* by Alexandre Luigini, Rimsky-Korsakov's *Scheherazade*, and the usual marches. Of course, it also played a lot of Mexican marches and some Mexican folk music. The folk music was especially difficult because it employed constantly changing time signatures—4/4 to 5/4 to 6/8, etc.

By the time we finally left, Leretta and I were already planning a return visit to Oaxaca the next summer. All through that year we corresponded with Seniors Baltazar and Mota, and I sent them some music they had asked me to get for them. Then as soon as my summer band program was over in July the two of us headed south for Mexico and our new friends. We had hardly settled in our hotel the first night in Oaxaca when Senior Baltazar appeared, and this time he brought with him Senior James Diego Innes, the senior conductor of the band. Along, also, came a reporter and a photographer from the local paper to do a story on me. In one year I had gone from gringo tourist to visiting fireman.

Senior Innes was an interesting man and a fine musician. His English first-name had been given him in honor of his grandfather, an Englishman who had settled in Mexico and married a Mexican girl. The family had money, and when James Diego was sixteen they had sent him to California to study the violin. He stayed there and got his American citizenship and finally became the director of the Milwaukee Symphony Orchestra. When the Great Depression came he had returned to Mexico where he was made head of the music department at the local university and the director of the Oaxaca State Band.

Once again my friends insisted that I stay two Sundays in Oaxaca and guest-conduct at the concerts, and I also rehearsed the band again at the convent. By this time I was beginning to learn some things about the Mexican approach to music. The Mexicans do not use the German A, B, C, D, system of naming the notes but the *solfeggio* system, that is, do, re, mi, fa, sol, etc. This is not our *solfeggio* system, where do is the tonic note of the key, but a fixed system in which do is always what we call C. For a while when I directed the rehearsals of the Oaxaca State Band I kept the names of the notes in this system written on a little slip of paper on my stand.

For a number of years after that, Leretta and I made one and sometimes two trips to Oaxaca every summer. Seniors Mota, Baltazar, and Innes especially became our good friends. Priscilliano Mota was an exceptionally cultured man, and after a short time we became almost like brothers. He had a charming wife and a fine son who could speak fairly good English. Whenever Leretta and I came to town we would always be invited out to his little house to sip a cool drink and eat *casadillas*, delicious little biscuits with Oaxacan white cheese inside. We would sit and talk music, which was the one big interest in Mota's life. I also visited Innes regularly, and he made several trips to see me in West Frankfort where he guest-conducted my band.

I wrote two marches for the Oaxaca State Band. The first one I gave to them as a kind of surprise on one of my visits. I had named it "Amigos Siempre" (Friends Forever), but Priscilliano Mota said, "We are more than friends," so we called it "Compañeros Oaxaqueños" (Oaxacan Comrades). The second

I called "Sol de Oaxaca" (Sun of Oaxaca). I named it partly in honor of the wonderful climate that exists so much of the year in Oaxaca and partly with reference to the well-known Spanish march "Sol a Seville." The State Band was still playing both marches when I went back there in 1979.

All in all, Leretta and I visited Oaxaca over twenty times. On one occasion I took the score and parts to Camilla de Nardis' *Universal Judgment* tone poem for the band to play. They were delighted with it, and Innes scheduled it for a Sunday concert during a festival. As we were rehearsing it, the bishop of the cathedral happened to be listening. When we came to the section in which the trumpets come in with strong chords like the tolling of bells, he stopped the band.

"I have an idea," he said. "Why don't I have the cathedral bells chime when you come to that part in the concert. Just give me a score. I have a couple of boys in the cathedral school who are working on degrees in music. They'll ring the bells."

I had my doubts about the plan, because there was no chance to practice with the bell ringers. If those loud bells came in in the wrong place, we'd have chaos, but Innes told me not to worry.

"They'll come in right," he predicted. "If the bishop orders it, you can bet it'll be right."

That Sunday we played *Universal Judgment,* and right on cue in came the cathedral bells. *Universal Judgment* is an impressive number the way it's usually played, but with those magnificent bells pealing away it really did sound like the Second Coming and the end of the world all rolled into one, and it just bowled everybody over. It made that concert one that the band, the audience, and I never forgot.

My visits to Oaxaca were some of the happiest times in my life. In addition to the stimulation of travel and of talking with people who thought and felt the same way I did about music, my trips gave me the chance to continue to play and hear the type of music with which I had been brought up. The movement away from the classics of the concert band repertory that grew faster and faster in the States after the war had not reached southern Mexico yet, and when I went down there, I was in a way musically coming home.

Today, of course, even Oaxaca has changed. It is over a hundred thousand in population now and much more tourist oriented. The State Band is still there, however, playing its Sunday concerts in the square, and it still programs some of the old numbers. Priscilliano Mota and Mozis Baltazar have both passed away, and Diego Innes died in 1985. In October 1984 I was fortunate enough to make one more trip down to see him. We spent two glorious weeks "batching" it in his little house in a tiny village just south of Oaxaca. There we listened to, and talked about, music from morning to night. With him as with me music has always come first, and for him it came last as well.

T·E·N

AS I LOOK back on those years that I spent as a music teacher in West Frankfort I can honestly say that they give me a good deal of satisfaction. There were troubles and rough times certainly, but the good things that happened outnumbered the bad by so many that there's no point in counting. I loved teaching, I loved young people, and I loved music, and in West Frankfort I had the chance to combine all those loves. What more can anyone ask of a career than that he be allowed to do the things that he loves?

Of course, one element that made my whole career worthwhile was the students that I taught. I haven't said much about individual students in this book so far, but right here and now I want to thank every single child I've taught over the years for making my job so satisfying. A number of my pupils went on to have satisfying careers in music; most of the others were successful in other areas; some are back with me now playing in the Southern Illinois Concert Band that I direct. But all of them from the most outstanding soloist to the most inept last-chair player did their share to make my music programs a success. I had so many good students that it's hard and probably unfair to single out names, but a few do stand out in my mind for one reason or another. I hope those whom I don't mention will forgive me. I loved you all. There was always a family spirit in my bands, and you were in a great sense all my children.

When I first came to town in 1930 there was a boy named Sylvester Parrigin who could play a little on the bugle. Sylvester became a very fine trumpet player and went on to study music at Vandercook College after he graduated from high school. He then went to Central City, Missouri, where he became an Episcopalian minister. He never lost his love for music, however, and continued to lead and play in bands. I still hear from him every once in a while.

One of my best early pupils was a little girl who played saxophone, Marcella Laws. Marcella's father sold one of his shotguns to buy her a gold-plated instrument, and she took first place in many state solo contests those first years. Although her instrument was alto sax, she was always willing to have a go at any saxophone we needed in the band and often played tenor and baritone sax when we were short of players on those instruments. She has also kept up her playing and still plays in three bands today.

Probably the most interesting student in that early band was Vade C. Davis. Vade was a rather strange boy, and before I came he had had some discipline problems. He just didn't seem to be interested in school or really in much of anything. I started him out on D-flat piccolo, and right away he found a purpose in life. He began carrying that piccolo around with him everywhere and practicing it constantly. He used to sit down on the curb on Main Street, prop his music up in the gutter, and practice. He became a fine flutist and won a number of first places in the solo contests. His discipline problems cleared up at the same time.

Another boy for whom music made a big difference and who developed into one of my favorite pupils was La Verne Sanders. I first got to know La Verne when he was only in the third grade. This was just after I had taken over the grade school band and we used to hold our rehearsals in the basement of the Central School. As the year progressed I began to notice that every once in a while a little boy would be sitting in the back listening to our practice. I checked around and found out that his teachers considered him a discipline problem, and when he'd cause a fuss they'd send him down to listen to the band because that kept him quiet.

90

Then one day I came down to the band room to set up the chairs for practice, and they were already in perfect formation. "Sonny," as evryone called La Verne in those days, was sitting in his usual place with an expectant look on his face. I asked the janitor who happened to be passing through if he had set up the band.

"No," he said, "it must have been Sonny."

After that La Verne always had all the chairs carefully arranged for me before every rehearsal. Then one day he came up to me with a battered old clarinet in his hand.

"I want you to teach me to play this, please," he said shyly. "I want to be in the band."

I told him I'd see what I could do. In those days I always gave a preband aptitude test to all the third graders just to determine if they had any musical ability at all. I dug La Verne's test out of the files, and there was a great big red zero on it. He hadn't gotten a single question right. The next day when Sonny came to band I told him maybe he'd better think again about trying to be a clarinet player.

The poor boy seemed terribly disappointed, but he kept coming to band and setting up the chairs, and every once in a while he'd pester me about letting him try to play clarinet. Finally, I relented. I always figured that if a child really wanted to play an instrument, I'd do my darndest to see that he got the chance no matter how much natural ability he did or didn't have.

La Verne Sanders took clarinet lessons from me all through grade school and high school. By the time he had graduated he was a pretty fair clarinet player. He also became sort of my right-hand man. He continued to set up the band and also put out the music. By the time he was in high school I was letting him take over some of the band rehearsals. He even started giving clarinet lessons on his own. All his discipline problems had long since cleared up. After high school he went on to earn a B.A. degree in music from Vandercook College, and later he got an M.A. degree in philosophy. I can safely say that La Verne Sanders was a boy for whom music opened up the world.

A number of my students have gone on to highly satisfying careers in music. One of my flute players, Charles Bolin, is now head of the music department at Illinois State University in Normal. Another of my flutists, Philip Eigenmann, has been the band director at Marion, Illinois, for many years, while Jean Barker, sax and oboe (who played for a time with the Chicago Women's Symphony), succeeded me as band director in West Frankfort. I was told a year or so ago that I have two former students playing professionally in Las Vegas, but I have never learned their names.

So many faces come back to me with affection. There was one of my best flute pupils, Myrtle Cox, who later became a teacher in West Frankfort High School. I remember little Tommy Graham, an outstanding clarinetist, and William Prusaczyk who excelled on that instrument. And I can't forget Ralph Schaffer, a very fine drummer who won a first place at the national solo contest. There was also my national contest-winning horn quartet made up of Glendine Purcell, Julia Henson, Paul Howard, and Dorothy Crem. There was Jimmy Wentworth and Lester Bristow who both won at the national contest on sousaphone. Jimmy was one of four Wentworth children who went through my program. His younger sister Phyllis won several firsts at the state level on bassoon.

And I mustn't forget Mary Greenwood. Mary started out playing the clarinet and did fairly well, but one year we needed bass horns in the high school band.

"If you'll give me one of those big things, I'll take it home and learn to play the damned thing," Mary told me.

I said I didn't approve of her choice of adjectives, but she could certainly have a go at the sousaphone. She soon became better on it than she ever had been on the clarinet. In fact, her father called me up one night and said, "You've got to do something. All Mary does is blow that damned horn, and I can't get any sleep!"

Mary had one peculiarity. She always kicked her shoes off when she played. She said she couldn't play well when anything made her uncomfortable, and tight shoes bothered her. Mary went on to major in music in college and for many years taught both vocal and instrumental music in Rantoul, Illinois.

One of my most gratifying experiences recently has been the number of my former pupils who have come back to play for me again in the Southern Illinois Concert Band that we formed in West Frankfort in 1983. They have all become my dear friends now, of course, and it is so gratifying to see all those seeds that I planted long ago still bearing fruit. I want to thank each of them: Mary Jane Stanhouse who plays oboe, Byford Young, one of our trumpets, Dorothy Dugger, our first French horn, and Donald Champion who had not touched his baritone horn in thirty-three years and has now come back to hold down a baritone chair. And I want to extend a special word of appreciation to Robert Treece who plays flute. Bob and his family have been my special friends and have gone out of their way to help me out and look after me these last few years. He has really taken the place of the son I lost so many years ago. And finally, I have to give a lot of thanks to my daughter, Bea, who now manages our music store and is right there playing bass clarinet in the band. Band directors' children have an especially hard time in music. They are expected to set an example for others in musicianship and practicing, but even more they are expected to fill in when the director is short an instrument. Bea always met the challenge. Any band director would be lucky to have such a daughter.

These are just a few of the students who made my teaching career so rewarding. There was a tremendous amount of latent musical talent in this area when I came. The people were hungry for culture, and music was one of the means by which they felt they could obtain it and pass it along to their children. Thus I had the full support of most of the parents and the school administrators, and music quickly became one of the most important activities in the West Frankfort school system.

Today, of course, the situation is different. There are many activities competing for children's attention that we didn't have in the thirties and forties. And there isn't the parental support that I enjoyed. In my time the parents made sure their children got to band rehearsals and often came themselves just to listen. Now, many of them don't even know when band rehearsals are scheduled, and they feel they are doing something if they come to one band concert a year.

Today many parents, school adminstrators, and school board members look on the band as only something to provide entertainment for half time at football games. Athletics has completely dominated their thinking. In my day bands did very little marching; we concentrated on the concert band, because this is where the children really learn musicianship. Now band directors have to concentrate on march flair and showmanship rather than on teaching the children their fundamentals.

This is not a very happy state of affairs, and its effects can be seen in the thousands of musically and culturally illiterate people our public schools turn out every year. But I also think that the music educators themselves must shoulder some of the blame for what has happened. We have been very effective in driving nails into our own musical coffins.

I think part of the trouble today is that many school band directors are not as dedicated as we directors were in my day. When I was teaching I lived music twenty-four hours a day, and so did most of my colleagues. In fact, that's almost all we talked about. Maybe we were narrow, but if our children didn't learn it was not because we didn't try. Today too many band directors want to forget about music when school lets out at three-thirty. They are more interested in the size of their checks than in the progress of their students. I am not saying that teachers should not be well paid, but a person should teach because he loves his subject and young people, not because he wants to make a quick killing.

When I taught I not only respected the teaching profession, I also respected music. I didn't just want my children to be able to play their instruments; I wanted them to play music, and I tried to pick good music for them to play. In those days there was no music written especially for the various grade levels and student abilities. There was just music. Some of it was easy, some was difficult, but all of it was written not to serve as some kind of teaching device but to create a certain kind of beauty. It was written for itself alone.

One of the major reasons the general public has abandoned the school band is that so much of the music programmed by modern school band directors is, pure and simple, crap. That isn't a very pretty word, but that's what it is. It may be technically demanding and sound flashy, but it is musically uninteresting and artistically dull. It may impress other band directors, but it turns off the public, and worse yet, it turns off our students. How can we expect our children to love good music, when all we give them to play is junk?

I think a lot of this problem goes back to the mid-thirties. In those days there wasn't a large repertory for the concert band. Bands played mostly transcriptions of orchestra numbers. Some band directors and musicians got the idea that this was a bad situation, and maybe in part it was. It may have been that we overdid the playing of standards like the *Light Cavalry* and *William Tell* overtures simply because there wasn't that much else to play.

But the pendulum quickly swung the other way. It became the aim of every band director to play only works written expressly for the concert band. Transcriptions in any form were out. And it soon became possible to program this way, because a number of enterprising composers began to write for the band. Some of them were good; many were not, but they churned out the material, and they are still churning it out today. It wasn't long before the band director who programmed the *William Tell* Overture was almost laughed out of the contest hall.

Now as I see it, there have been at least two bad effects from the prejudice against transcriptions by music educators. First, abandoning the classics has cut our students off from the great traditions of our Western musical heritage. Like it or not, most of the serious music of the last five hundred years has been written for orchestra. The band director who refuses to play transcriptions is automatically refusing to recognize this heritage, and he is doing nothing to teach it to his students. There is nothing like playing a piece of music, even in transcription, to gain an understanding of it and a love for it. And there is nothing like hearing at a concert or over the radio a number you yourself have played to stir a love for music.

Second, by programming music that no one but other band directors ever listen to, the music educators alienated the natural audience for the band. The concert band began as a popular, middle-class institution. In the first chapter of this book I mentioned that when I was a boy John Philip Sousa's "King Cotton" march was a popular tune of the day. The people who thronged to the band concerts in the park for the first fifty years of this century had primarily middle-class tastes. They were willing to listen to selections from Verdi operas now and then as long as there was some familiar light music liberally mixed in.

When band directors started pleasing and impressing each other and stopped programming music their natural audience knew and loved, they turned off that audience. And it is this audience that still for the most part provides the children who make up our school bands. When I was teaching, a school band concert was a big event. People came to hear the music, not simply because it was expected of them as parents. Now, too often for too many parents a band concert is an ordeal. They come and listen to this strange stuff, music they have never heard before and will never hear again, and they are bored. Can we really expect these people to take an active interest in our music programs if the only time they can relate to the music the band plays is when it is marching at a football game?

I am not saying that there have not been many fine compositions written for the concert band and that these should not be programmed. It is just that so many band directors have lost all sense of proportion. Unless a number has been written expressly for concert band in the last ten years, they won't play it. Does this really make sense? How long would a symphony orchestra stay in business if it programmed nothing but twentieth-century works all the time. It is a rare orchestra that dares to play even one concert a season dedicated exclusively to modern music. Yet if you are going to play only "band music," you are going to have to look long and hard to find much material that was written before 1900. And ironically, even the numbers that were written for band—the marches of Sousa, Goldman, and King, for example—are considered passé by modern band directors.

Sometimes I think I must sound like an old crank when I preach on this subject of music education. But, you see, I have to speak out, because I feel it is so vitally important. Our young people need music; they need all the arts, and if no one works to see that they get the instruction they need, we will have raised a generation cut off from one of the most important influences in making people civilized and human. This will be a terrible tragedy, and we can't allow it to happen.

After all, look at what music has done for me. I am over eighty years old, and today I am a happy man. Oh, I've certainly had my share of trouble. I lost my son in a tragic accident; my dear wife Leretta died; my second wife is incapacitated. But still I am happy and I've always been happy, because I've had my music. I thank God that I can still take my baton and call forth those marvelous melodies that have been with me since I sat in my little chair so long ago and listened to my grandmother teach her piano students. Often when the Southern Illinois Concert Band plays a passage extra well, I get tears in my eyes from pure joy.

I have always been a religious man, although not much of a churchgoer. I find God through nature, and I have a reverence for all of life. I guess I got some of this from old Hale Vandercook. But I also believe that human beings can come to God through beauty, especially the beauty of music. Thus if we cut our young people off from music, we are really cutting them off from what is most important in human life. We are denying them a chance for the religious experience that gives meaning to life. To do this to a whole generation would be a tragedy indeed.

But today I am optimistic. There is starting to be a renewed interest all over the country in the great band music of the past. The progress we have made here in southern Illinois is being repeated in many other places. Since we have formed our band to play the old standards, I have had letters from friends and colleagues everywhere congratulating us and wishing us well. The American Association of Concert Bands has been formed to further the community band and band music. Many of the young bandmasters I have talked with are enthusiastic about the old music, and school music educators are starting to program more intelligently. And if the bandmasters come back, the public is going to come back, too. You can see that in the audiences we draw to our Southern Illinois Concert Band concerts.

Today as I look back on my life I can't help feeling that much of it was directed by a higher power. So often things had a strange way of working out just when it seemed my life was completely stalled. When the theaters closed down and there seemed to be no more room for me in the music profession, what happened? I came to West Frankfort intending to stay only a month, and I ended up spending the rest of my life here. Just as my career as a school band director was coming to a close, my music store business began to blossom. And now near the end of my life a group of people from all over the area have come to me and asked me to do the one thing I love to do best, direct them in a concert band.

And thus I am very happy. I still live in my own house with the many cats I love to take care of. I still listen to, teach, and conduct my music. And I still have my printing hobby. I print all of the programs for the Southern Illinois Concert Band on the press in my garage, using the type that I have collected through the years. My friends are around me. Lucky, you say? Maybe. But maybe I have a higher power to thank.

Whatever the case, there is one thing I know. All the greatest happiness I've had in my life has come to me through music. I have never been sorry that I dedicated my life to it. Even in my darkest periods it has sustained and strengthened me. It has always demanded the best I could give it, but it has always repaid my efforts a hundredfold. I guess if you were to sum up my life, it would take only one simple sentence. "Ted Paschedag was a musician." In the course of my life I have been many other things, too: a printer, a businessman, a teacher, and a traveler, but through it all and above it all, with Ted Paschedag, the music always came first.

THOMAS J. HATTON was born and brought up in Fort Dodge, Iowa, where as a young man he played saxophone in a band directed by the famous circus band director and march composer, Karl L. King. Hatton earned a B.A. degree from Buena Vista College and M.A. and Ph.D degrees from the University of Nebraska, specializing in Middle English literature. An associate professor in the English department of Southern Illinois University, Carbondale, Hatton has published several articles on medieval literature, a biography of Karl King, a book on playwriting, and over twenty plays and short stories. He continues to maintain an active interest in music and music performance, having served on the Executive Board of the Herrin Federation of Musicians and playing saxophone in the Murphysboro, Illinois, Municipal Band and the Southern Illinois Concert Band directed by Ted Paschedag. Hatton lives in Carterville, Illinois, with his wife, Lois.

Marcha "Compañeros Oaxaqueños" F. W. Pascal